CONTENTS

PART TWO: GCP AND GLP

PREFACE

Those participating in clinical research that is either intended for regulatory purposes or sponsored by the Medical Research Council (UK) and other government bodies, are now usually required to conduct all aspects of the studies in accordance with Good Clinical Practice. This small book was written to provide an accessible but comprehensive summary of the latest guidelines with respect to Good Clinical Practice, ethics review procedures and Good Laboratory Practice. It is aimed at the aspiring 'investigator', whether working in primary care or hospital, medical or nursing research. I hope it will be useful either alone or as an adjunct to GCP training courses. In addition to outlining the principles of GCP, as agreed by the International Conference on Harmonisation and by the Medical Research Council, the book contains practical ideas about implementation, and some brief information on trial designs and trial patient management.

Many excellent texts have been written about research methodology and an increasing number are being written about drug development, but very few concern the interaction between clinical staff and research sponsors during a clinical trial. Much of the material in this book is based on twenty years personal experience of collaboration with clinical investigators throughout Europe. On listening to them, it sometimes seems that the demands of sponsors are burdensome and bureaucratic. I believe it doesn't have to be that way.

Good Clinical Practice has been devised to improve standards and confidence in clinical research. Sensibly applied, the principles should assist researchers in achieving these aims.

Ann Raven
Cambridge Healthcare Research
October 1998

ACKNOWLEDGEMENTS
The author wishes to thank Brenda Mullinger for editing the text, Juliet Corfield for preparing the manuscript and Mike Emanuel for helpful comments and kindly preparing a Foreword. She is also grateful to Jo Gardiner at Leverpress for her expertise and forbearance.

Foreword

The assessment of the safety and efficacy of medicines in clinical trials requires a marriage of the scientific research method with the science and practice of clinical medicine allied to the technical standards now known universally as Good Clinical Practice. All this has to be carried out within a regulatory framework which varies according to national regulations and the ethical standards encompassed on a world-wide basis in the Declaration of Helsinki.

The science and technology of clinical trials has led in recent years to the publication of a rich literature in the form of books, reviews and many research papers. The majority of these have been produced from the viewpoint and needs of the research sponsors, usually the pharmaceutical industry. A typical and excellent example is Ann Raven's 1991 book "Consider it Pure Joy... An Introduction to Clinical Trials", which gives a clear and simple account of the clinical trial process and the work of the sponsor's representative, the clinical research associate.

"Beyond What is Written... A Researcher's Guide to Good Clinical Practice" is an important addition to the literature of clinical trials. Successful clinical research is a true partnership between a sponsor and one or more clinical investigators. The sponsor and investigator hold joint responsibility for the science, ethics and quality of any research. Ann Raven's new book primarily addresses the basics of clinical trial methodology (including the relatively new area of outcomes research) and the processes required for Good Clinical Practice. The book is structured and the text is written from the perspective of the needs of the research investigator, whether they are doctor, nurse or pharmacist. The stated objective is "to provide an accessible but comprehensive summary of the latest guidelines in respect to Good Clinical Practice, ethics review procedures and Good Laboratory Practice".

The book provides important background reading and reference material for researchers in clinical medicine who regularly or occasionally work on clinical trials as well as those who wish to do so in the future. It will enhance the way that clinical investigators understand the needs and requirements of their industrial and public sector sponsors, and in that way lead to increased efficiency and standards in clinical research. Patients who consent to take part in clinical trials have the right to expect as much.

Mike Emanuel
R&D Director
Janssen-Cilag Ltd
October, 1998

PART ONE

CHAPTER 1

CLINICAL TRIAL DESIGN

Overcoming Bias in Clinical Trials
Run-in Periods and Pilot Studies
Randomised Controlled Trials
   Group Comparisons
   Crossover Studies
   Alternative Designs
Cohort Studies
Case-control Studies
Outcomes Research
   Clinical Efficacy and Effectiveness
   Safety Measures
   Quality of Life/Health Status
   Economic Evaluation
Phases of Clinical Development
Avoiding Duplication

Most clinical research employs those quantitative research designs that are most appropriate for answering the questions

– is this new treatment more effective than nothing/current normal practice?

– what effect does this intervention have on the patient in terms of side effects, quality of life, etc?

Many textbooks primarily focus on the randomised controlled trial (RCT) as the principal method for assessing new health technology, particularly new drugs. However, the increasing pressure to consider economic and quality of life outcomes, and to study new interventions under normal conditions, means that methods traditionally associated with epidemiology are also being used. In the following section, therefore, aspects of trial design such as mechanisms for removing bias and outcomes measures, will be discussed; the RCT will then be described, together with cohort, case-control and economic studies. Since many readers will be involved in drug evaluations, the recognised phases of clinical development will also be outlined.

Overcoming Bias in Clinical Trials

It is important in any trial to minimise the sources of bias. The most important mechanisms for doing this are through the use of controls, randomisation and blinding.

Introducing a control group immediately improves the strength of the trial design. Controls can be historical, such as a previous surgical series in the same hospital, but they suffer from the possibility that staff, infrastructure, patient management, casemix or other treatments may have changed. An historical control derived from published literature potentially suffers from publication bias, and any differences between the setting and circumstances of the published series and the present study. For these reasons most controls are arranged concurrently with the experimental group. Controls may involve the use of an active comparator (for instance the standard or reference (drug) treatment), a placebo or no treatment. Active comparators should be selected carefully; to permit a valid comparison they must be relevant to the trial population and equivalent in dose/strength/duration to the new drug, as far as can be reasonably deduced from pharmacology and previous experience. Placebo 'treatments' should be identical to the active treatment in appearance, smell, taste, weight etc, but lack the active substance.

The placebo response observed in a placebo controlled trial is a complex phenomenon and is not the same as the response in an untreated group. Placebo has been described as the "most effective medication known to science, subjected to more clinical trials than any other medicament yet nearly always does better than anticipated. The range of susceptible conditions appears to be limitless". The perceived placebo response comprises the true placebo response as well as the natural course of the disease, regression towards the mean, time effects (often related to investigator contact and trial procedure) and unidentified parallel interventions such as lifestyle or dietary changes. The true placebo effect depends upon such factors as the attitude of the doctor (towards the treatment or the patient), the attitude of the patient (towards health, the doctor or treatment), their suggestibility, and the type of treatment.

Randomisation helps to reduce possible allocation or selection bias and provides a sound statistical base for subsequent analysis. Simple randomisation involves the use of a random list or random number generator to allocate consecutive subjects to the various treatments to be compared. There are advantages to randomising patients in blocks of, for example, 6 or 12, to ensure that each treatment group will contain a similar number of patients. Ideally, researchers should be unaware of the block size to avoid being able to predict the allocation towards the end of a sequence.

If it is known that certain baseline characteristics of the patients may influence treatment outcome (e.g. disease severity, age, gender), it can be sensible to stratify the randomisation list to balance the treatment groups for these prognostic factors. Also, in multicentre trials it is common practice to have a separate random scheme for each centre. Multiple stratifications can be logistically complex. However, if it is considered important to include multiple factors, the use of minimisation or adaptive randomisation is possible. This method allocates a new patient to a treatment group depending on the current balance of subjects between groups. It has the advantage that, whenever the trial stops, it is likely that all treatment groups will be balanced with respect to those critical prognostic features which could be identified in advance. Invariably, minimisation involves the use of computer algorithms, often at a central site, so the logistics need to be considered carefully.

Blinding is intended to reduce possible bias in the selection of patients, their allocation to treatment, their subsequent clinical evaluation, the handling of withdrawals and other aspects of their management, which could occur if the researcher was aware of the treatment being received by an individual. A double-blind trial is one in which neither the investigator nor the patient is aware of the treatment received. In a commercially sponsored trial all those practically involved with the study will also remain blind until the database is clean and verified. Whilst a double-blind approach is generally considered ideal, it can be difficult to achieve in practice; for instance, when different treatment forms are to be compared, such as surgery and drug therapy or an injectable versus an oral drug. In some cases the use of a double-dummy technique is helpful – for this, both active and placebo supplies are prepared for each treatment and each subject receives an active of one and placebo of another. This enables the blindness to be maintained but may burden the patient with a complex regime and reduce treatment compliance. Dummy surgical procedures are also fraught with ethical dilemmas, and some may not be feasible. Sometimes, physiological effects of a treatment (such as facial flushing) may compromise the blindness of either the patient or the researcher.

When double-blind designs are not possible, single blind (either researcher or patient aware of the treatment) or open-label designs can be employed. Bias can still be minimised if clinical assessments are performed by medical staff not involved in treating patients, and if randomisation can be undertaken centrally, so that patients are selected and enrolled prior to treatment allocation. Any study related mechanism for the reduction in bias should be described and justified in the trial protocol.

Run-in periods and Pilot Studies

It may be helpful to include a run-in period at the beginning of the study, in some circumstances. Firstly to improve confidence in the diagnosis – there are some conditions, e.g. asthma, that cannot be diagnosed accurately on a single occasion – so a patient may be asked to record, e.g. peak flow, over a 1-2 week period and then return to the clinic. Secondly, a run-in can be useful to provide training in the assessment method, e.g. use of a diary card or a bicycle ergometer etc. A run-in may also serve as a washout period if patients need to stop taking other medication prior to entering a trial, either to avoid carryover effects or drug-drug interaction. It may be necessary to undertake this gradually over several days for safety reasons, and may help to establish an untreated baseline. Such a washout should be sufficient for 5 times the drug half-life. Finally, a run-in may help to identify non-compliant patients who are unable or unwilling to fulfil the needs of the study.

Pilot studies should be more widely employed and can be conducted for a number of reasons. They may be used to test the measurement technique, to examine the logistics, to improve recruitment estimates or to help define the patient population. Very often the data on the first few patients is compromised through unforeseen logistic or technical problems.

Randomised Controlled Trials

Randomised controlled trials (RCTs) are the most rigorous way of determining whether a cause and effect relation exists between treatment and outcome. In an RCT all groups are managed identically apart from the experimental treatment. Patients are randomly allocated to intervention groups and are usually analysed within that group (intention to treat analysis). RCTs are usually conducted in a double-blind manner, where feasible. It is assumed that prior to an RCT, researchers show equipoise – that is, genuine doubt about whether one treatment is better than another. Trials must be carefully designed to ensure they have sufficient power to detect a difference between treatment and control groups, if one exists, or to demonstrate there is no effect if the treatment is ineffective. The smaller the effect being sought, the larger the number of patients needed to detect it.

Group Comparison

The most common design for RCTs is a between patients comparison known as the group comparison or parallel group comparison. In this design a group of patients is randomly allocated to one of two or more treatment options under identical conditions, and the outcome of treatments compared, during and after a specified (and usually identical) treatment period. Every effort must be taken to render the patient groups comparable at the outset or baseline of the trial, and to control the conditions under which they are managed so that any differences in effect between the groups can be reasonably explained by the treatment received. Since the patient groups are involved in the study at the same time this should reduce any variation due to changes in climate, staff or institutional factors. Comparisons can be made at various times during the treatment period to establish, for example, whether one group had a more rapid resolution of symptoms, or a peak in adverse effects at a particular time. Also, comparisons in the health status at the end of treatment, or the change from baseline, can be made between the treatment groups. This design is usually the most suitable for acute conditions and is the preferred choice of all drug evaluation agencies.

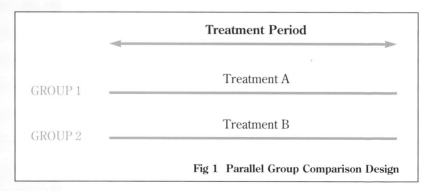

Fig 1 Parallel Group Comparison Design

Crossover Studies

In chronic, stable conditions and in particular where individual variation in treatment response is great, a within patient design can be employed, in which each patient/group receives each treatment option in random order and hence acts as their own control.

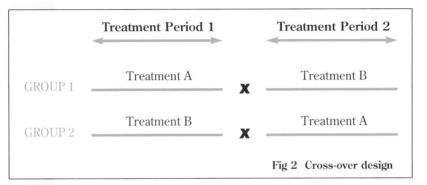

Fig 2 Cross-over design

This design requires half the number of patients of an equivalent group comparison design but each patient will be involved at least twice as long. The principal challenge of this design is the need to ensure that the patient's health status (eg severity) is stable at the outset of each treatment period so that each period can reasonably be compared. In practice, this is rarely achieved, often resulting in a drifting baseline. Also, it is difficult to prevent carryover effects from the first treatment into the second treatment period, thus rendering it difficult to attribute treatment responses. In theory, there should be a washout period at the crossover point, equivalent to five times the half-life of the trial drugs, to help minimise this effect and the possibility of drug-to-drug interactions. This can make for a very protracted study, particularly if there are three comparators, and therefore suffers from high patient attrition (or drop-outs). However, it has been used successfully in diseases such as angina and epilepsy, and is commonly employed in dose ranging and dose titration studies.

Alternative Designs

In an adaptation of the RCT, Zelen has proposed an alternative in which patients are randomised prior to giving consent – a group of patients are assigned standard therapy (control group) and the remainder asked to accept an experimental treatment – those refusing also joining the control group. This design is intended to improve external validity by increasing the proportion of patients enrolled, but has rarely been adopted to date. Another, more recent, suggestion is the incorporation of patient preference into trials of interventions where participation and motivation are necessary for the success of the treatment (this is rarely the case for drug trials).

Cohort Studies

Cohort studies are widely used in epidemiology research to investigate the incidence of events or disease and their cause.

A cohort or group of patients is observed over a period of time to establish, quite simply, what happens to the patients. Hitherto little used in healthcare research, the cohort study is growing in popularity as we seek to better understand the natural history of a disease – particularly referral patterns and resource use, and perhaps long-term adverse effects or wellbeing. The cohort study can be considered a form of prospective longitudinal survey, but the study still has to be designed rigorously, paying attention to the sample size, the period of follow-up and the outcome measures employed. The interpretation of cohort studies is also improved by the inclusion of a carefully selected control group. Such an observational design is often subject to over-enthusiastic interpretation and cohort studies are particularly prone to selection bias and losses to follow-up. They are generally less suitable for establishing effectiveness than an RCT, as the design will detect an association but not necessarily causality. However, they offer an excellent and relatively straightforward mechanism for answering questions about expected prognosis which in outcomes research can be of primary concern.

Case-control Studies

Another design associated with epidemiology, the traditional case-control study, compares people with a certain disease and those without it, with the aim of defining the relative contribution of one or several factors to the frequency of the disease. However, case-control studies can be used for a much wider range of questions, such as attitudes of users and non-users towards preventative healthcare, why some patients but not others respond to a treatment, or why some patients develop post-operative complications whilst others, experiencing the same operation, do not.

Because case-control studies are performed retrospectively they can be conducted relatively quickly and cheaply, and have the added advantage that they can investigate quite a range of differences between cases and controls in a single study. They are also ideal for investigating rare events since you start with the cases already identified. The success of these studies relies on rigorous case selection and well matched controls, giving due consideration to the care setting involved and proper sample size calculation. Also, since data are collected retrospectively, often by interview or questionnaire, there may be problems of differential recall. Even with case-note review it is important that data collection techniques are identical. Often, it is desirable to ensure the researcher is 'blind' as to whether the subject is a case or control, during data collection.

Outcomes Research

Until recently the focus of much medical and surgical research was the clinical and laboratory endpoints employed to define success or failure of an intervention. Now the outcome of a new drug treatment or operation is considered more broadly and may also include the quality of life changes for an individual patient and/or their family, or even the impact on the health service – perhaps in terms of resources such as numbers of inpatient days reduced or increase in monitoring visits, and hence costs.

Clinical Efficacy and Effectiveness

These two terms are sometimes used interchangeably but should be quite distinct; an efficacy study is designed to show whether a treatment can work, usually in ideal conditions, whereas effectiveness reflects whether it does work in normal practice. Sadly, but almost inevitably, these two often provide different results, so that a highly efficacious drug with unacceptable side-effects may prove ineffective in normal practice through poor patient compliance.

Efficacy needs to be established first, in carefully controlled conditions, usually with an RCT. Efficacy measures need to be chosen carefully; they must be clinically meaningful or, at least where surrogate endpoints are employed, the relationship between the measure and the clinical event (e.g. lipid levels and myocardial infarction) should be robust. Since many studies will be conducted at several different sites, efficacy measures should ideally be measured easily with accuracy and appropriate precision. The methodology should be widely accepted and valid for the care setting and population (this is particularly important for mental health rating scales). The measure of efficacy should also be sensitive to change over the anticipated period of study. As in any experiment, it is undesirable to be asking too many questions at once, so trying to establish a new measure of disease severity in the context of an efficacy trial of a new treatment is not ideal. Where this is unavoidable it is very important also to include a well established measure to provide concurrent validity. In all clinical trials the urge to measure too many parameters should be resisted – not only to avoid any unnecessary costs (from measurement, analysis, etc.) and burden to the patient, but also because if the trial becomes too complex it is easy to lose sight of the primary measure and hence compromise the whole exercise.

Clinical efficacy trials are necessarily artificial experiments. They involve very careful monitoring of specially selected patients, often in the very best clinical environment. Trial patients are motivated to take their drugs carefully and have many extra safety tests. Often, many of the visits and tests would not happen in normal clinical practice, so clinical trial settings tend to produce increased use of healthcare resources (costs) and also better efficacy results.

Once absolute efficacy is established, however, it is important to widen the selection criteria and evaluate a new intervention in more normal circumstances to establish true effectiveness. This is particularly important for cost-effectiveness studies.

Safety Measures
It is vital that any subject involved in research is adequately protected by appropriate safety monitoring. The degree and number of tests will depend on the phase of development and the nature of the intervention. There is often a tension between the desire to protect and the burden to the patient, and researcher, of repeated venepunctures, urine tests, biopsies or other interventions. It is also important to avoid non-essential tests which not only increase costs but also require follow-up in the event of abnormality – and, naturally, the probability of a chance result outside the normal range increases with the number of tests. This applies both to pre-treatment tests, establishing study eligibility, as well as to those made during or post-treatment.

Quality of Life/Health Status
An intervention which improves clinical status but reduces overall quality of life may not be a positive outcome, whilst a

treatment which has minimal effect on illness severity but substantially improves quality of life, may be much appreciated by both patients and healthcare professionals alike. In clinical research it is increasingly common to differentiate treatments using health-related quality of life scales. Some are disease specific, such as the EORTC-QLQ used in cancer, while others are more generic, such as Euroqol or SF-36. Instruments have been developed which cover domains such as physical and social functions, emotional status, cognition and perception of own health; other scales focus on dimensions of distress and disability, and some measure the impact of disease on Activities of Daily Living. Such measures are particularly important in the evaluation of patients with chronic disease.

Generic instruments permit comparisons across different types of intervention and conditions. Research into preferences for certain health states have enabled the development of scales used in economic evaluations to derive Quality-Adjusted Life Years (QALYs), a composite measure of quantity and quality of life. The cost per QALY for a particular intervention can then be compared with cost per QALY for a quite different type of treatment.

Economic Evaluation

Economic evaluation provides a means of comparing the health resource implications of alternative treatments and management systems, by considering the various healthcare 'inputs' (e.g. drugs, doctor's time, hospital beds) and consequences (e.g. improvement in health or avoidance of an undesirable event such as a heart attack). Economic evaluations vary in their perspective; they may aim to reflect the viewpoint of society, which would involve health care, social services and family inputs, together with health and financial consequences and impacts on productivity. Alternatively, an evaluation may adopt a particular health care perspective looking at costs and consequences for the hospital sector and not considering the effect on social services' resources or patients' own costs. All economic evaluations involve measuring the inputs and the outcomes and then giving each a value, for two or more competing treatments.

The most common form of economic evaluation today is the cost-effectiveness analysis in which outcome or effect of two treatments can be measured in the same units (e.g. number of infections resolved by antibiotics) and then the costs expressed as cost per unit outcome (e.g. cost per infection resolved). If the outcome of different treatments proves to be the same, only the costs need to be considered and this is then called a cost-minimisation analysis - the aim being to identify the cheapest effective treatment.Cost benefit analysis is used when both inputs and outcomes of different treatments can be expressed in financial terms. Cost utility analysis is used when the treatments to be compared have different outcomes in terms of quantity (i.e. length) and quality of life. These studies measure the amount of 'utility' or value derived from the treatment by the patient, often using QALYs, and this type of analysis compares the cost per QALY of each treatment. This form of economic evaluation is very useful when, for example, a health authority must decide on which patients to spend scarce resources (or money). Perhaps the authority wants to know whether heart transplants or kidney dialysis provide the best value for money for the local population. A cost-utility analysis can help determine priorities based on the cost per QALY of each treatment.

Increasingly, governments and commercial sponsors of clinical trials are seeking an economic evaluation of a new treatment, often by including it in Phase III and Phase IV studies. Whereas randomised clinical trials are designed to test efficacy and safety, as discussed earlier, this necessarily artificial set-up is not ideal for economic analysis. Even so, methodologies for incorporating economic analysis alongside clinical trials are currently being developed both in industry and academia.

Outcomes research, which encompasses clinical, economic and social outcomes of treatments, is likely to become a growth area within healthcare research over the next few years.

Phases of Clinical Development

Traditionally, health technology assessment, notably of drugs, has referred to four temporal phases. Whilst the content of each phase is not fixed and does not describe the study design it can be helpful to recognise the objectives and features of each phase. The following section accords with the International Conference on Harmonisation (ICH) guidance on drug development (ICH E8, 1997; for details, see Appendix).

Phase I (Human Pharmacology)

The objectives of the first studies in humans are:
1)   initial safety and tolerability
2)   preliminary pharmacokinetics.

The studies are usually conducted in healthy volunteers but for drugs with significant toxicity, such as cytotoxics, studies are conducted in patients. They include single and multiple dose administration and aim to provide guidance on the dose range suitable for clinical studies in safety terms. Drug-drug interactions and specialised pharmacokinetics (e.g. in the elderly or renally impaired) are usually conducted later in development but are still termed Phase I.

Phase II (Exploratory Therapeutic)

These studies are typically the first ones in patients and their objective is to explore therapeutic efficacy. At this stage it is also hoped to establish a dose-response relationship and gauge the safety in a relatively small number of patients. A well-defined group of patients is closely monitored in relatively short term studies. It is considered important to evaluate suitable study endpoints and the most appropriate target population at this stage. Invariably, placebo controlled evidence of efficacy will be needed to justify progression to Phase III.

Phase III (Confirmatory Therapeutic)

These studies often involve a large number (thousands) of patients and aim to confirm the therapeutic potential of a new drug/intervention. In addition, the objectives include a safety evaluation in the selected patient population at a duration of exposure equivalent to the intended 'normal' use. This will provide a profile of adverse reactions. Together, Phase III studies should provide a basis for a marketing approval and therefore include studies in the wider population, at different stages of the disease and in comparison with existing treatments. Invariably, Phase III studies are double-blind, randomised controlled trials, employing common efficacy and safety parameters. Often the development programme for a new treatment will be conducted in many countries so studies need to be standardised to facilitate evaluation. Studies on new clinical indications for already marketed products are also termed Phase III.

Phase IV (Therapeutic Use)

These studies are conducted after market approval and are limited to the licensed indication for that product. They are often important in establishing the optimal use of a new drug/technology and may include long term safety, comparative efficacy, epidemiology studies in special populations (geriatric or ethnic groups) or pragmatic effectiveness studies. Economic evaluations are often conducted at this stage.

Avoiding Duplication

In an attempt to help researchers avoid inappropriate duplication of effort and research on patients, several registers of ongoing research have been created in recent years. Time spent establishing whether similar work is ongoing is usually a good investment, and discovery of similar studies may positively inform the study design. In the UK, the National Research Register has been under development for several years and can be accessed via a CD-ROM produced by the NHS R&D Directorate. In addition, there are several national and international directories of clinical trials and both the Centre for Health Economics, York and the Office of Health Economics produce a database of economic evaluations. MRC funded projects can be easily identified from their website and most medical charities and Trusts produce informative lists of ongoing and recently completed projects. The challenge to the researcher is to know whether these registers are comprehensive. Currently this is not the case except for particular funders – in particular, most commercial sponsors do not release this information. This situation can only improve and will be assisted if researchers ensure that their own research is entered on the appropriate register at the outset.

CHAPTER 2

PATIENT RECRUITMENT AND MANAGEMENT

Estimating Patient Numbers
Patient Recruitment Strategies
Addressing Slow Recruitment
Premature Withdrawals
Keeping Patient Records

Estimating patient numbers

In any clinical trial it is important for the researcher and sponsor to agree that the patients/subjects as defined in the protocol are appropriate for the clinical site. Ideally, these patients will be presenting or be referred in a routine way. If the patients as defined are atypical or need bringing to the investigating site through special means, the study will be more difficult both to conduct and to schedule. Most investigators are able to provide retrospective data (eg audit or routine clinic records), showing that patients of the required diagnosis, age-group and severity are available at that site. These data can be used to justify an anticipated recruitment period to the sponsor and ethics committee. (In the absence of such data it may be useful to employ the trial selection checklist for a month or two to identify the number of potentially eligible patients.)

Patient Recruitment Strategies

GCP guidance makes it clear that the investigator is responsible for ensuring access to an adequate and appropriate source of subjects for a trial, but it says little about how this should be achieved. As already mentioned, before embarking on a trial the potential availability of suitable subjects is demonstrated on records, previous similar trials or a review of case notes. Armed with this information and the numbers of patients required from that centre, the recruitment period can be agreed, and thence weekly or monthly recruitment goals calculated. Frequently, these goals need to be adjusted to take account of staff holidays, clinic closures, training, conferences and the like. Over-optimistic estimates are rarely helpful, especially as patient consent to a trial may be unpredictable.

Once the numbers and schedule have been established a recruitment strategy should be considered – and agreed with the sponsor. The strategy will include raising awareness amongst colleagues and the patient group, and will list the mechanisms for identifying potential subjects (e.g. for chronic conditions, recall of existing patients). In addition, the actual enrolment procedures must be carefully addressed, identifying who will conduct initial examinations and screening tests, explain the trial to patients and obtain informed consent. The consent process needs to be done in a relaxed, unhurried manner and may not be achievable in the midst of a busy clinic; if patients feel flustered they are less likely to give consent. Often, permission must be sought for screening tests before eligibility for the study can be determined and full informed consent obtained. This may lead to a two-visit enrolment:

1) check general suitability and conduct screening tests and make subsequent appointment (to research clinic);

2) on receipt of test results, undertake thorough examination and obtain informed consent.

Naturally, such a strategy will depend on the nature of the tests; sometimes it will be more appropriate to obtain informed consent before any trial-related interviews are undertaken.

It is vital at this stage to agree a reasonable reporting period for any mandatory safety tests to be conducted before a patient receives a trial intervention. Many a patient has been lost to a trial through late reporting of screening results.

When scheduling trial visits, consideration should be given to the patient population – are they elderly and frail, with possible transport difficulties or a desire to be home before dark? Or are they a younger group in employment who may need early morning or evening appointments? Sometimes the trial itself will restrict the choices by requiring, for example, overnight fasting and therefore early morning visits. Efforts should be made to anticipate obstacles to patient enrolment, and common sense may suggest providing taxi fares for the elderly patient in rural districts, or breakfast for the 'overnight faster' on the way to work.

Whatever recruitment procedures are adopted, the logistics should be agreed by all the site staff involved before the study begins and also communicated to the ethics committee.

Addressing Slow Recruitment

The reasons for difficult or slow recruitment of subjects are legion and invariably specific to the trial or site. The experienced investigator will plan carefully to avoid over-promising and ensure smooth recruitment of the required number of subjects. S/he will also consider in advance what action to take if initial recruitment is disappointing. If the protocol is well constructed and reviewed as appropriate for the site, the commonest problems are logistics and communications at the site.

Clearly, selection criteria should have been reviewed carefully in advance, but if all selection checklists are collated, this will reveal if a particular criterion is responsible for excluding many patients. The value of this criterion can then be reviewed in the light of patient safety and trial objectives.

A few common problems associated with slow recruitment are listed below:

C No suitable patients presenting:
   problem with selection criteria?
   initial bad luck?
   seasonal fluctuation?
   inadequate predictions from retrospective data?
   changes (in staff/clinics/wards) at investigator site?
   changes in local referral patterns (e.g. new regional centre opened)?

C Suitable patients presenting but failing screening:
   too restrictive screening test?
   site patient population not matched to protocol?

C Suitable patients presenting but not agreeing to participate:
   problem with trial – too burdensome/risky?
   problem with consent process/written material?
   investigator too busy?

C Suitable patients presenting to clinic but not to trial investigator:
   lack of referral by colleagues to investigator?
   lack of awareness of trial amongst clinical staff?
   investigator not available?
   recruitment strategy not communicated to colleagues?
   other competing trials in department now underway?

Some of these problems are more susceptible to solutions than others. The issue of colleague awareness is predictable and can be addressed in a variety of ways:

- letters to colleagues (at outset and later) explaining objectives of research, selection criteria and requesting assistance;
- holding a lunchtime meeting to describe intervention and trial to colleagues;
- giving a presentation at local journal club/postgraduate centre followed by verbal request for referrals;
- direct approaches to other members of clinical team who may be aware of suitable patients, e.g. nurses, health visitors, technicians;
- advertising a trial on clinic noticeboard (only acceptable in some circumstances);
- when patient enrollment is delegated to a junior, ensure that principal investigator is providing full support – in practical ways;
- for chronic diseases, arrange search of patient records and recall/write to potentially suitable cases. A meeting could be held for such patients at which the trial is described and patients invited to attend for screening;
- where a clinic nurse allocates new outpatients, provide a sheet of key selection criteria (and flagging slips) so that suitable patients are routed to the investigating doctor.

Sometimes a clinic seems awash with potentially suitable patients for the trial but none of them seem willing to participate. Research into the reasons why patients do or do not agree to enrol in studies is limited. Much depends on the culture and personality of the patient and often the investigator too; sometimes the very kindest doctors are unable to enrol patients into placebo controlled trials. Certainly, if the doctor or nurse is anxious about the trial interventions or procedures themselves, often that is somehow relayed to the patient. However, the following suggestions may encourage participation:

- ensure patients are interviewed in a private, quiet environment in an unhurried manner;
- suggest that patients take information sheets away to discuss with their families before deciding;
- review and rewrite patient information in a more acceptable, or accessible, language or involve a nurse in the consent process;
- suggest patients visit the clinic for a demonstration of the measurement techniques; often the equipment considered routine by clinic staff may be perceived as alarming or dangerous by patients;

- arrange, where possible, for patients happily involved in a trial to be available to talk to new patients about their experience of the procedures;

- review the burdens of the trial for individual patients and where possible schedule visits to suit them or consider home visits, etc.;

- where clinic appointments are often delayed, assure trial patients that they will be seen promptly for trial visits (e.g. by reserving the first appointment in a session for them, or setting up separate research clinics);

- allay anxieties amongst site personnel (if a member of the trial team is unhappy with the trial).

When recruitment is slow it behoves the investigator to discuss the situation with the clinic staff and the trial sponsor (who will usually provide a trial manager or a monitor to help with study conduct – see Chapter 11).

Premature Withdrawals

Sometimes, patient recruitment meets the target but only a few patients go on to complete the trial period. This can be very disturbing, not least because of all the time and effort the investigators and patients have invested in the trial, especially if the data will not then permit conclusions to be drawn. Whilst patients are naturally free to withdraw at any time, the investigator should aim to enable patients to complete the trial unless, of course, they are suffering ill effects. There are a number of possible explanations for premature withdrawal which merit consideration:

- genuine treatment failure; when the new intervention fails to provide an adequate response after a reasonable time, it may be impossible to justify a patient continuing in the trial (depending on the indication);

- the treatment is successful; the patient feels better and decides to stop visiting their doctor;

- the condition resolves and the patient declines further treatment;

- patients dislike the trial procedures (e.g. endoscopy, repeated venepunctures);

- patients dislike a member of the investigating team and withdraw co-operation;

- patients dislike the intervention (e.g. an appliance which is uncomfortable, a drug which tastes bad, an injection which is painful);

- trial visits are too frequent and inconvenient or the trial is simply too long;
- adverse events (AEs) occur; even apparently mild and non-serious AEs will, if persistent, lead to the patient withdrawing early.

Whatever the reason for premature withdrawal, the investigator must record it carefully – it may prove to be the principal outcome of the trial, e.g. the intervention could not be tolerated sufficiently to evaluate its efficacy. There is often an element of 'Loss to follow-up' in which patients vote with their feet and fail to return to visit the researcher. The main problem is usually lack of information as to why the patient did not return. Is she recovered? Worse? Suffering from debilitating adverse effects? Or has she moved away, lost her diary card or simply got bored with the demands of repeated assessments? If the numbers lost to the trial in this way become substantial it threatens the validity of the study. In GCP trials the investigator is obliged to make every effort to establish the reason for withdrawal.

Whenever problems occur in a multicentre study there should be an opportunity for investigators to share information; particularly successful strategies in one centre could be of value elsewhere. Often sponsors will facilitate this process via monitors, a trial steering group or joint investigator meetings.

Patient Record Keeping

During the study the investigator must arrange to keep careful records of each patient's involvement and progress in the trial. The trial register, code-breaker envelopes (if appropriate) and signed consent forms must be stored carefully and a record made on case notes that the patient is involved in the trial and the date enrolled. The patient should be provided with an ID or appointment card showing their trial number and the trial identification in case of an emergency. Where permission is given, the patient's primary care doctor should be informed of their involvement in a trial at a hospital or clinic.

Throughout the study the case record form should be completed and maintained up to date, and key information recorded in the patient's case notes (e.g. dates of visits, drugs prescribed, critical test results and any adverse events) for both safety and verification purposes.

CHAPTER 3

RESEARCH FUNDERS AND CLINICAL TRIALS

Sources of Funding
   National Health Service, Department of Health and MRC
   Medical Research Charities and Trusts
   Commercial Sponsors
Liaison with Pharmaceutical Sponsors
   Resources Required for Clinical Trials
   Globalisation of the Pharmaceutical Industry
Contract Research Organisations
Studies in General Practice
Co-investigators and Study Site Co-ordinators
Joint Investigator Meetings
Multinational Studies

Sources of Funding

Financial support for clinical research is most readily available in the form of grants from a wide range of funding bodies – each with its own preferences for topics and research methods. It is important to match the project to the funding body at an early stage, and informal contacts can prove very helpful to assess suitability.

Sometimes it is difficult to know where to apply. The following section provides a very brief summary of some options for the UK. Contact details are included in the Appendix.

National Health Service, Department of Health and Medical Research Council

The NHS launched an R&D initiative in 1991, which established a number of research programmes in topics such as:

Mental health
Cardiovascular disease and stroke
Cancer
Primary and Secondary Care Interface

which fund a wide variation of research projects. In addition, there is the Health Technology Assessment Programme, the largest NHS programme, which includes diagnostics, surgical, pharmaceutical, screening and methodology sections (contact details are included in the Appendix). Each programme posts calls for applications to conduct research on specific topics, according to their priorities, in leading medical journals, such as BMJ. Each region of the NHS also has local research funds which are awarded on the basis of merit and usefulness to the NHS with 2 or 3 submission deadlines per year.

The Department of Health in each UK country also disburse funds and, although much of the work is commissioned, they will consider researchers' own projects.

The Medical Research Council is the leading funding body supporting substantial health services research. There is an increased emphasis on large-scale multidisciplinary research, but they also provide training fellowships, institutional grants and short term funding for innovative research. Competition is fierce as particular prestige is attached to MRC grants. Details of their programmes and applications are freely available.

Medical Research Charities and Trusts

Medical charities play a major role in supporting research – the largest being the Wellcome Trust, with an annual budget in 1998 of £150million, which will consider applications on any topic except AIDS and cancer. Next are the larger charities focused on a specific disease, such as the Cancer Research Campaign, British Heart Foundation and the Arthritis and Rheumatism Council. There are hosts of other and smaller charities, all with separate policies for funding and application procedures. Details of all these can be obtained from the Association of Medical Research Charities Handbook – details in Appendix.

Most hospital trusts and health authorities have R&D managers who will advise on local and national funding opportunities. Other sources include the European Commission which funds major multinational collaborative research, the Economic and Social Research Council (ESRC) which, as its name suggests, funds primarily sociological, psychological or economic research.

Most professional societies, including colleges or nursing and medicine, have funds available for research.

There is such a plethora of funding sources that it may be useful to consult the Wellcome Trust Wisdom Search website which contains details of over 300 sources which can be searched using subject area and key words.

Commercial Sponsors

Drug and device manufacturers sponsor about half of all UK clinical research. Whilst much of the research will be related to their products in development, most companies also support substantial numbers of projects in related areas of medicine. Sponsorship tends to be provided for those researchers already known to the company. It can be a challenge to know which company to approach – the Association of British Pharmaceutical Industry (ABPI) may be able to help.

Funding bodies usually provide detailed instructions and application forms for the preparation of research protocols and grant applications. The reader is referred to an excellent Pocket Guide to Grant Applications recently published by BMJ Books – details in Appendix.

Liaison with Pharmaceutical Sponsors

Why would a physician or nurse choose to involve themselves in a commercially- sponsored clinical research programme? Many individuals and groups are motivated purely by a desire to be involved in evaluating better treatments. Some need to increase departmental income. There may be many other individual benefits to becoming a clinical investigator, which include maintaining academic interests in therapeutics, increased contact and exchange of ideas with peers from different areas or countries, opportunities to travel to academic conferences to present/discuss new treatments, and career advancement. There is no question that some form of ongoing research is motivating for both clinical staff and for patients, particularly in those areas where, so far, there is little of therapeutic benefit available for the patient.

Pharmaceutical companies rarely provide candidate drugs directly to clinicians who wish to conduct their own studies. Although, in the UK at least, it is possible for doctors to obtain permission to conduct independent research with unregistered drugs according to their own protocols, such requests are more likely to be met with an invitation to be part of a more formal and regulated drug development programme. This is not to say that drug companies are necessarily unwelcoming to direct approaches from physicians - just that the regulations surrounding the supply of candidate drugs outwith a formal clinical trials programme mitigate against such projects.

It is more common for the investigator to be approached by a sponsor or drug company with an invitation to participate in a trial. Drug company staff, often a physician or monitor working in the medical, or research and development (R&D) divisions, may appear to be extremely inquisitive and even probing about the suitability of the department, clinic or investigator. However, it is, of course, a partnership they are seeking, in which both parties should not only benefit, but also reach mutual agreement on how the research will be conducted.

Research amongst investigators into the factors that affect successful collaboration with drug companies shows that the individual relationship between the investigator and the monitor is critical. If investigators feel that the individual co-ordinating the research project is competent, communicating clearly both the requirements of the company and all pertinent drug related information, and empowered to make and keep to commitments concerning contracts, schedules, provision of emergency advice and reporting, then the level of trust engendered will make for a successful collaboration.

So, investigators and their colleagues who will be involved in a potential project should assure themselves that they will be entirely comfortable with their potential 'partner', namely the sponsor company. Questions worth asking are:

- is the initial information on the drug comprehensive (and reassuring)?
- is the protocol clear and feasible in this setting/culture?
- are the company staff well informed, easily contacted and well organised?
- are the requirements of the company and the needs of the investigator clearly laid out in an agreement?
- is the company interested in the clinical expertise being offered?
- is the financial arrangement commensurate with the effort and time involved?

There will inevitably be one or more meetings with company representatives so there should be ample opportunity to consider whether the research is sufficiently attractive for an involvement that may span several years.

Resources Required

Potential investigators should also consider carefully the demands of a clinical trial, particularly one run to GCP standards. Since the trial represents an additional burden on resources, an outpatient clinic which normally runs smoothly can be seriously disrupted by a major clinical trial. This may be because of the time needed for initial screening and explanation of the procedures before obtaining consent, or because more frequent follow-up visits upset the normal throughput of patients. Also, if unexpected adverse events occur, requiring additional monitoring and consultations, staff may become over-stretched. Even the storage of study materials, special dispensing of blinded pharmaceuticals or requesting medical records for an additional (non-NHS) clinic can cause friction amongst busy colleagues.

As a result the principal investigator needs to consider carefully the resources needed to conduct each aspect of the study and consult with anyone who needs to co-operate, such as pharmacy, medical records, phlebotomy, laboratory and technical staff, as well as clinical and nursing colleagues. Sometimes, a diagnostic service such as endoscopy or bone-scanning can be overwhelmed by a new clinical trial. It is usually possible to anticipate where the workload will fall, and, if recruitment of patients can be predicted confidently, also the schedule of activity so that, if necessary, staffing levels can be adjusted accordingly. Sometimes, a special clinic set up for clinical trial patients can save many organisational headaches, providing that all the support services find this convenient. Investigators must be able to demonstrate that they have the time and space for additional interviews and examinations, and appropriate secure storage for equipment, case records, drugs and code-breakers and the like.

Also, for studies run under GCP that involve equipment and/or laboratory processes, these need to be shown to be organised, maintained and documented. Therefore, an investigator may expect to be asked to demonstrate that staff have adequate and relevant training and the equipment itself has records of maintenance, calibration and written methods. The details of how this is best achieved are included in Chapter 12 (Laboratories and Good Laboratory Practice). In addition, for haematology and biochemistry safety test normal ranges will be required, for a population relevant to the trial patients, and information concerning quality assurance (QA) schemes should be provided to the sponsor. Health service and private 'central' laboratories are usually run to high standards and regulated nationally, via accreditation schemes, so these requirements should not be an additional burden. However, for the primary care or independent doctor these necessary systems may be new.

Delays in recruitment are among the commonest problems in clinical trials, and can lead to tensions between the sponsor and investigator site, so time spent producing a realistic estimate based on the selection criteria always proves a wise investment – and should always be done before the trial supplies arrive! The sponsor will request recent CVs from all investigators (i.e. anyone with a key role at the site) and also wish to establish that they understand the rigours of trial conduct and their responsibilities under GCP (see Chapter 5 for a complete list).

Globalisation of the Pharmaceutical Industry

Pharmaceutical companies have been experiencing a proving time lately, as price controls limit profits, and escalating demands and costs of pre-registration research are threatening their viability. This has resulted in a plethora of acquisitions, mergers, and increased licensing of candidate drugs to other companies. For the clinical investigator this is potentially both confusing and disruptive, as research priorities and policies often change with new management. Also, the focus on R&D productivity has led to the widespread use of contract research organisations (CROs) and freelance/contract staff to co-ordinate and analyse clinical trials.

Some companies are well established in some therapeutic areas and have a high profile and track record in their drug development. It is natural to feel more confident that their research programmes will be well conceived and managed. It is good to remember that the research and marketing arms of a company may be very separate, both in terms of management and culture.

In addition, due to the globalisation of development programmes, often international trials are being co-ordinated from the US or Japan where previously more local, national studies were undertaken. This may lead to some apparently 'foreign' design features, diagnostic criteria or assessment methodology, as companies attempt to standardise their clinical development across many cultures and medical traditions. This problem many become acute if the parent company perceives medicine as more of a business than a profession, with the result that there appears to be an unattractive rigidity and one-sided authority in the relationship. Not surprisingly, this approach is rarely successful in Europe where physicians' involvement in clinical trials is not bought but negotiated.

Another feature of drug development is the increasing number of Central and Eastern European companies now developing their own compounds in North Western Europe as they seek alternative markets. Many of these companies are relatively unknown in the West although products of their research laboratories have been successfully marketed here for years, by licensors. These companies may have excellent facilities and be conversant with the procedures for obtaining permission to import and evaluate new medicines in Western Europe. They may also be well aware of the financial needs and pharmacovigilance systems necessary to run a high quality programme.

All this produces a confusing picture for the new investigator. Who is making the decisions? With whom is the contract made? Where is the real expertise about this new drug? These are important questions for investigators to ask before embarking on a new trial, quite apart from the more obvious ones relating to scientific interest and medical need.

Contract Research Organisations

A Contract Research Organisation (CRO) or contract monitor will have a legally binding contract with the trial sponsor which will clearly delineate roles and responsibilities with respect to trial design, monitoring and data analysis. CRO staff are usually highly motivated to run a study efficiently and on schedule and one can expect them to have excellent research methodology and organisational skills. In theory, they should be as informed as sponsor staff about the pharmacology and development of a new drug, but in practice they may be less aware of international strategy and the pharmaco-vigilance reports, and may have less opportunity to become deeply knowledgeable about a specific therapeutic area. Researchers need to ensure that they are receiving drug information updates and advice from the sponsor to the same extent as if they were collaborating directly – in particular with the responsible clinician. It is also sensible to be especially clear when negotiating financial contracts with CROs.

Contract monitors may be employed by a sponsor to overcome short to medium term staff shortages. Often they will work from home and may have fewer administrative resources than sponsor staff, but this is usually balanced by many years experience of monitoring.

Studies in General Practice

Traditionally, early phase research, with the necessary emphasis on safety monitoring, has been easier to conduct in hospitals where laboratories and specialist equipment are more accessible and where there are better facilities for emergencies. However, the well equipped health centre of today can handle most clinical trials very competently, providing the protocol is appropriate and the staff have been adequately trained. With the increasing number of patients being treated in a primary care setting, drug companies need to do more clinical trials on candidate drugs with general practitioners.

It is important that the sponsor recognises that the GP may have less time per consultation and so may need a shorter CRF than might be employed in an outpatient setting. Mechanisms may be required for preparing and despatching biological samples to central laboratories and ensuring prompt reporting. Whilst most modern practices have ECG machines, sphygmomanometers, and the like, it may be helpful to arrange for specialist interpretation of some screening or safety tests.

Since the GP is obliged to be away from his clinic much of the time, it is particularly important that the patient's notes clearly show their involvement in a trial and colleagues should be aware of the protocol and the location of code-breakers. As in any trial, the patient must carry a trial ID card with their physician's emergency contact number. Sometimes, in cases where it could be predicted that a patient might have an emergency admission (such as asthma or angina trials), it may even be appropriate (or required by the ethics committee) for the local hospital to be informed about the study schedule and protocol.

On occasion, the diagnostic expertise required by the protocol will not be available in general practice. In these instances it is often more satisfactory for a specialist to visit the health centre regularly and conduct the study in partnership with the GP. This is usually preferable to all the patients travelling to the hospital and will reduce the number of drop-outs.

Storage of documentation, drugs, biological sampling supplies and extra equipment may cause problems to a GP in shared accommodation. Most companies can provide assistance by delivering smaller quantities of supplies at a time and by more regularly collecting returned or unused drugs.

The administrative burden of clinical trials, especially since the advent of GCP, may be difficult for a busy general practice. A GP must be really sure that they have the time, and staff support, to conduct a trial safely, on schedule and to GCP standards. In addition, the sponsor should provide adequate monitoring support with appropriately trained staff.

Co-investigators and Study Site Co-ordinators

At each site there is one principal investigator who bears legal responsibility for the conduct of the trial and the delegation and supervision of all other staff. However, the value of a trial is often enhanced by a team approach and in many trials the complexity of the assessments and safety monitoring will entail the involvement of many other doctors and technical staff. It is important therefore that these colleagues are fully aware of the objectives of the trial and are kept informed about all aspects of progress. Thus, the head of laboratories, medical physicist, radiographer or pharmacist may be co-investigators in addition to physician or surgeon colleagues and junior medical staff. It is helpful if all names and contact numbers are provided on the protocol, and ideally all parties should meet together, with the sponsor, before any trial begins, to ensure i) the study is feasible at the site in respect of each party's workload and resources and ii) communication lines (e.g. for screening, referrals, sampling) are clear.

A study-site co-ordinator (SSC), identified as the contact person or co-ordinator for all activities at that site, be it hospital or general practice, and who may be a physician, nurse or scientist, will keep the sponsor appraised of progress or any problems. In addition, they will be responsible for maintaining all the trial documentation including case record forms (CRFs), and collaborating with monitors and auditors from the sponsor company.

On most occasions, the involvement of an SSC immeasurably improves the quality both of patient follow-up and data, and their appointment is much favoured by sponsor companies.

Commercial and academic training courses for SSCs are now widely advertised and, in the UK, study site co-ordinators may join the Association of Clinical Research for the Pharmaceutical Industry which provides several educational opportunities and a forum for improving understanding between investigators and drug companies (see Appendix for contact details).

Joint Investigator Meetings

Very few clinical studies are conducted in single centres since the numbers of patients required are usually too high for a single group to recruit within a reasonable time. Collaborative, multicentre studies are therefore commonplace. For large collaborative studies, it is sensible for all investigators to meet together and agree on all aspects of the protocol. Sponsors very often organise joint investigator meetings in the planning stage of the project to discuss:

- diagnostic criteria
- other patient selection criteria
- measurement / assessment procedures
- visit schedules
- CRF design

These meetings, usually attended by principal investigators, provide an opportunity for the sponsor to explain and describe the drug's development to date, and to discuss the requirements of GCP, monitoring procedures, the possibility of audit and any other relevant practical issues. They also provide an occasion for investigators to raise any areas of concern with senior R&D staff from the sponsor company.

Sometimes, a meeting is arranged after the protocol is finalised with the objective of agreeing:

- recruitment strategy
- inter-rater reliability
- CRF completion procedures
- data management issues
- any other practical, logistical arrangements.

When subjective assessments are employed, as in psychiatry, it is particularly important to ensure that different investigators interpret and score signs and symptoms in a comparable manner. This can be achieved through repeated rating of the same patient on video interview, or using photographs, or, where appropriate, through teaching on the relevant scale by an 'expert'. Any variations are discussed until all present have reduced their rating variability to an acceptable level. Obviously, it is important that the investigators attending these meetings are those who will actually assess the patients, not necessarily the 'principal' investigator.

Generally, sponsors arrange these meetings in a convenient location and cover all investigator's costs relating to their attendance. It is vital that afterwards investigators promptly receive a report of the meeting, including all agreements made and action steps of all involved.

Multinational Studies

Multistate applications for product licences for candidate drugs within Europe, and the desire by major companies to globalise the development process, have increased the number of multinational studies, particularly in the hospital sector.

International collaboration is far from new but investigators need to be aware of the pitfalls of multinational clinical trials. Naturally, the difficulties will vary enormously between disciplines and countries, but in general one can expect complications in the following areas:

Diagnosis:	variation in terminology, differential diagnoses, relative importance of symptoms.
Presentation/ Recruitment Strategy:	health systems vary and also patterns of presentation. What is appropriate for one country may prove impractical in another.
Comparators:	in comparative efficacy trials difficulties in agreeing upon one standard reference drug, dosage and regime, as comparator.
Culture:	laws concerning consent, confidentiality and access to records reflect different cultures and attitudes. Also insurance, diet, religion, relationship with doctors and other social factors can impact on the study conduct.

Assessment:	availability, application and experience of clinical measurement techniques may vary between countries.
Routine treatment:	Policies for hospital admission, length of stay, frequency of patient contacts, use of other therapies (including drugs) and tests are all likely to vary across national boundaries.
Regulatory procedures:	permission to proceed with clinical trials is sometimes easily forthcoming, but procedures vary between countries. Investigators may be beginning their part of the study 6 months after colleagues overseas or substantially earlier. This is particularly frustrating at the end of an exciting project, when it results in a long wait for the analysis. In Phase III trials, a new drug may be marketed in some countries before others, which may cause difficulties. As rules for drug import/export are variable, delays to trial supplies that are beyond the sponsor's control may occur.

Overcoming these and other problems is, of course, certainly possible but may require a degree of compromise on all sides to produce a mutually acceptable trial protocol. Usually the sponsor will initiate the necessary dialogue with investigators, and they often invite a well respected opinion leader to chair the discussions.

CHAPTER 4

REGULATION OF CLINICAL TRIALS

Ethics Committees
  **National Multicentre and Local Ethics Committees
  – a new UK system**
Informed Consent
Clinical Trial Authorisation

Ethics Committees

All clinical trials require the prior approval of the appropriate ethics committee. No subject can be enrolled into a trial until written approval from the ethics committee has been received. Researchers should be aware of the operations of their local or institutional ethics committee and also the regional/national committees. The expectations of GCP on both the researcher and the independent ethics committee are clear but demanding, and it is of great value to develop a positive relationship with the local committee.

To be compliant with GCP an ethics committee should consist of at least five members of whom at least one should be a non-scientist and another should be independent of the trial site or institution. Between them they should have sufficient expertise to evaluate the science, medical aspects and ethics of a clinical trial. The committee should have written procedures and keep good records of all meetings, and maintain records for up to three years after the trial is completed. It is not acceptable for members absent from a review meeting to proffer an opinion or advise on a particular protocol (e.g. by telephone or post). Sponsors may request a list of members and written procedures.

Researchers need to submit the following documents to the appropriate ethics committee:

- Trial protocol (including amendments)
- Investigator brochure
- Informed consent form
- Subject information sheet
- Recruitment procedures (e.g. advertisements)
- Investigators' CV
- Information concerning payments/compensation to subjects.

On occasions the ethics committee may also require a copy of the letter to be sent to the subject's family doctor and other, additional, information at their discretion. Frequently they will enquire about any financial arrangements between the researcher and the sponsor. A local, institutional ethics committee will consider not only the merits of the trial but also the experience of the researcher and the capacity and facilities of the site to conduct such a trial.

Investigators take responsibility not only for the initial submission (in some circumstances they will need to attend the meeting to answer questions/promote the trial) but also for keeping the ethics committee informed of progress and untoward events. Annual reports must be sent to the ethics committee, detailing progress in terms of recruitment, completion and adverse events. In addition, unexpected serious adverse events should be reported promptly to the ethics committee together with any safety information that arises during the study which could influence the safety of trial subjects or their informed consent. Finally, at the end of the trial the investigator should inform the ethics committee of the completion date and outcome.

Careful records should be kept of all correspondence with ethics committees; these will be subject to inspection from both research funders and possibly national government audit staff. It is good practice to identify dates/versions of any document sent to any ethics committee, to avoid confusion.

National Multicentre and Local Ethics Committees – a new UK system

GCP requires that each country provide a national ethics committee able to review protocols and give an opinion promptly. Some countries have had operational national review ethics committees for some years whilst others, such as the UK, have only recently introduced a network of regional multicentre research ethics committees (MRECs), which can act as a national ethics committee for large studies.

The perspective of national or multicentre research ethics committees is necessarily focused on the wider scientific and ethical issues presented by a particular research protocol. A local research ethics committee (LREC) is particularly interested in local resources and the ability of the investigator and their colleagues to cope with the additional burden of the trial.

In the UK, when research is to take place in more than five areas covered by LRECs, it is necessary to obtain approval from an MREC first. There are eight MRECs in England, one for each NHS region, and one each in Scotland, Northern Ireland and Wales. When an existing study is extended to more than five centres, approval from an MREC must also be sought, although the LREC approvals for the original centres will still be valid.

MRECs require a substantial fee for commercially-sponsored research and some LRECs also charge fees. Whilst the 300 UK LRECs are currently very varied in terms of composition and working practices, the MREC system is now very clearly defined. Each MREC has an administrator and publishes submission deadlines and meeting dates. They acknowledge receipt of all submissions and advise of decisions, in writing, within 10 working days of the meeting. On occasions, researchers may be invited to attend the meeting.

It is necessary to complete a comprehensive MREC application form; this currently runs to 15 pages and is available on the internet, along with comprehensive guidance for applicants (see Contact details in the Appendix). The LREC has no power to change the protocol once an MREC has approved it, but may, at present, change patient information sheets. If one LREC rejects a multicentre study protocol then the other LRECs and MREC administrator must be informed. Submission is usually by the principal (clinical) investigator in the study to their regional MREC, although some MREC submissions are arranged by sponsors.

Once an MREC approval has been granted, the local researchers may then each approach the relevant LREC to gain local approval. The LRECs should receive both the MREC application form, response form and approval, consent and information sheets and the protocol (and investigator brochure).

A new directive on GCP in clinical trials will become law in most European countries in the next two years. This calls for national ethics committees to provide an opinion within 30 days of receipt of a valid application.

Informed Consent

Researchers have a key role in ensuring that all subjects are fully informed about the project and are able to give and document proper consent. The process originates with the Declaration of Helsinki, which is endorsed by GCP.

In addition to a thorough verbal explanation of the study, the patient should be provided with a written information sheet so that they can consider carefully what is involved, and the alternatives. The way in which information is presented to subjects will have a great influence on the recruitment into a study. Researchers should compose or review any written information carefully to ensure the language is appropriate and accessible to their patients. In some cases it is sensible to show patients the diagnostic or measurement equipment or arrange for them to speak to other patients who have experienced the trial, to allay anxieties. Always, the consent process needs to be unhurried and relaxed. Many authorities recommend that patients have at least 24 hours to consider their involvement in a clinical trial. Box A lists the information which must be provided to the subject, as specified by ICH GCP.

The researcher also needs to answer any questions the subject might have. Obviously, informed consent must be obtained prior to any involvement in the trial. The consent form should be signed by both the subject and the person who conducted the consent discussion, and dated. This form should be retained at the trial site, and may be inspected but not removed by monitors from the sponsor organisation.

If, at any stage of the study, the procedures or safety information available change in such a way as to influence the original consent, it may be necessary to update the information sheet and consent form and inform the patient accordingly. Any such revisions require prior approval by the ethics committee.

Clinical Trial Authorisation

In addition to ethical approval, researchers need to obtain management approval from their institution before embarking on a project involving public health service facilities.

Where studies involve new and unlicensed pharmaceuticals, permission to conduct clinical trials must be sought from the national licensing authority. Usually this is undertaken by the sponsor, but the researcher should ensure they have a copy of such approval before starting a trial (ethics committees will also request a copy).

Informed Consent: Necessary Information for trial subjects   A

a) That the trial involves research.

b) The purpose of the trial.

c) The trial treatment(s) and the probability for random assignment to each treatment.

d) The trial procedures to be followed, including all invasive procedures.

e) The subject's responsibilities.

f) Those aspects of the trial that are experimental.

g) The reasonably foreseeable risks or inconveniences to the subject and, when applicable, to an embryo, foetus or nursing infant.

h) The reasonably expected benefits. When there is no intended clinical benefit to the subject, the subject should be made aware of this.

i) The alternative procedure(s) or course(s) of treatment that may be available to the subject; the subject should be made aware of this.

j) The compensation and/or treatment available to the subject in the event of trial-related injury.

k) The anticipated prorated payment, if any, to the subject for participating in the trial.

l) The anticipated expenses, if any, to the subject for participating in the trial.

m) That the subject's participation in the trial is voluntary and that the subject may refuse to participate or withdraw from the trial, at any time, without penalty or loss of benefits to which the subject is otherwise entitled.

n) That the monitor(s), the auditor(s), the IRB/IEC and the regulatory authority(ies) will be granted direct access to the subject's original medical records for verification of clinical trial procedures and/or data, without violating the confidentiality of the subject, to the extent permitted by the applicable laws and regulations and that, by signing a written informed consent form, the subject or the subject's legally acceptable representative is authorising such access.

o) That records identifying the subject will be kept confidential and, to the extent permitted by the applicable laws and/or regulations, will not be made publicly available. If the results of the trial are published, the subject's identity will remain confidential.

p) That the subject or the subject's legally acceptable representative will be informed in a timely manner if information becomes available that may be relevant to the subject's willingness to continue participation in the trial.

q) The person(s) to contact for further information regarding the trial and the rights of trial subjects, and whom to contact in the event of trial-related injury.

r) The foreseeable circumstances and/or reasons under which the subject's participation in the trial may be terminated.

In the UK there is a two-tier system. Pharmaceutical companies may either apply for a Clinical Trial Certificate (CTC), in which the Medicines Control Agency (MCA) reviews a full dossier of pre-clinical information (this often takes nine months to process), or an Exemption from Clinical Trial Certificate (CTX) in which only a summary dossier is submitted and a decision is available in 28 days. Clinical trial approval is also required when a trial is exploring a new and unlicensed indication for a marketed drug or device.

It is possible for an independent researcher to be granted permission to conduct a trial with an experimental drug by applying directly to the MCA under the "Doctor's Direct Exemption" (DDX) scheme and requesting appropriate supplies from a pharmaceutical company. In practice, this is now quite unusual.

Most countries have an equivalent national system for authorising clinical trials.

PART TWO

CHAPTER 5

GOOD CLINICAL PRACTICE

Introduction
Benefits of GCP
Investigators' Responsibilities
Ethics Committee and Sponsors' Responsibilities

Introduction

Originally, Good Clinical Practice (GCP) was a set of proposals prepared and published in 1977 for the guidance of investigators and drug companies undertaking clinical trials in the US. They were prepared as a response to anxieties about the quality and reliability of some of the research data submitted to the regulatory authorities. Similar guidance also exists for Good Manufacturing Practice (GMP) and Good Laboratory Practice (GLP).

Good Clinical Practice is defined as an international, ethical and scientific quality standard for designing, conducting, recording and reporting trials that involve the participation of human subjects. Compliance with this standard provides public assurance that the rights, safety and well-being of trial subjects are protected, consistent with the principles that have their origin in the Declaration of Helsinki and that the clinical trial data are credible.

The main tenets of the GCP proposals are that clinical trials should be good science, verifiable, monitored, well documented and complying with high ethical standards. Although not initially popular even in the country of origin, GCP has now been accepted by both drug companies and many government funders and is the required standard for drug development aimed at international product licences. Some European investigators found the initial guidance rather unacceptable, but in 1991 an EC working party published European GCP guidelines and these are now widely implemented. More recently the International Conference on Harmonisation (ICH) has achieved a harmonisation of the GCP guidelines developed in Japan, the US and Europe and the resultant ICH GCP guidelines now have legal status in most EU countries. In the UK they have been largely adopted by the Medical Research Council (MRC) and other government research funding bodies.

The objective of the International Conference on Harmonisation is to provide unified standards for the EU, Japan and US to facilitate mutual acceptance of clinical data by regulatory authorities. A copy of the ICH GCP guidelines can be obtained from the ICH Secretariat (address in Appendix) or via the Internet. The MRC has produced a GCP booklet for all its researchers and now routinely audit trials to ensure compliance with these standards. The principles of GCP are listed in Box B.

Principles of GCP   B

1. Clinical trials should be conducted in accordance with the ethical principles that have their origin in the Declaration of Helsinki and that are consistent with GCP and the applicable regulatory requirement(s).

2. Before a trial is initiated, foreseeable risks and inconveniences should be weighed against the anticipated benefit for the individual trial subject and society. A trial should be initiated and continued only if the anticipated benefits justify the risks.

3. The rights, safety, and well-being of the trial subjects are the most important considerations and should prevail over interests of science and society.

4. The available non-clinical and clinical information on an investigational product should be adequate to support the proposed clinical trial.

5. Clinical trials should be scientifically sound, and described in a clear, detailed protocol.

6. A trial should be conducted in compliance with the protocol that has received prior institutional review board (IRB)/independent ethics committee (IEC) approval/favourable opinion.

7. The medical care given to, and medical decisions made on behalf of, subjects should always be the responsibility of a qualified physician or, when appropriate, of a qualified dentist.

8. Each individual involved in conducting a trial should be qualified by education, training, and experience to perform his or her respective task(s).

9. Freely given informed consent should be obtained from every subject prior to clinical trial participation.

10. All clinical trial information should be recorded, handled, and stored in a way that allows its accurate reporting, interpretation and verification.

11. The confidentiality of records that could identify subjects should be protected, respecting the privacy and confidentiality rules in accordance with the applicable regulatory requirement(s).

12. Investigational products should be manufactured, handled, and stored in accordance with applicable good manufacturing practice (GMP). They should be used in accordance with the approved protocol.

13. Systems with procedures that assure the quality of every aspect of the trial should be implemented.

These principles have led to practical guidelines encompassing the following topics:

- ethics committees and informed consent
- the selection of investigators
- protocol content
- drug accountability
- trial monitoring, data validation and source data verification
- adverse event reporting
- data handling, use of computers and statistical analysis
- content of trial reports and investigator brochures
- archiving CRFs and trial documentation
- standard operating procedures (SOPs) and quality assurance

They are primarily organised under headings of Ethics Committee, Investigator and Sponsor (drug company) responsibilities. Part Two of this book concerns the theory and practical implementation of ICH GCP for research doctors and nurses or investigators.

Benefits of GCP

Benefits of GCP and GLP include increased confidence in the data, better quality trial designs, a standardised approach and one development process.

Developing drugs and other new technologies is an expensive and lengthy business; it may cost £100 million and take more than 12 years to develop one licensed drug. It is undesirable to repeat the process in different parts of the world. Therefore it is a sound idea to ensure that the research data are acceptable to all national regulatory authorities. Since the US is the largest single market for pharmaceuticals, most drug companies wish to be successful there. The US Food and Drug Administration (FDA) will review clinical trial data only if the trial has been conducted to GCP standards.

The implementation of GCP guidelines is, without doubt, improving the quality of clinical trials sponsored by drug companies and reviewed by government agencies, and the harmonised approach is a major advantage for both industry and the research community.

Investigators' responsibilities

Any clinical researcher who takes responsibility for conducting a clinical trial sponsored by the industry or funded by the MRC is entitled an 'investigator'. The principal investigator has overall legal responsibility for the study and may delegate different aspects of the study conduct to co-investigators such as junior doctors, pharmacists, nurses or laboratory researchers. It is not unusual for a study site–co-ordinator, often a research–trained nurse, to conduct most of the day-to-day activities of the trial, but management oversight by a senior clinician is required. Investigators' responsibilities are encompassed in 12 sub-sections of the guidelines which are explained more fully in later chapters but can be summarised as follows:

1. Medical researchers undertaking clinical trials must be **suitably qualified** 'by education, training and experience' to undertake a specific study. This applies not only to the principle investigator but also to their colleagues. Personnel records need to be maintained and provided to the sponsor (or funding institution) before the trial starts. Investigators must also appraise themselves fully of the nature of the study protocol and the experimental drug (or material).

2. The site selected to conduct a trial should be able to demonstrate **adequate facilities** to conduct the study safely and efficiently in respect of, for example, equipment and suitable accommodation. The site also needs staff with sufficient (spare) time and access to an appropriate population of patients from which to recruit subjects for the trial.

3. The investigator must ensure that all trial subjects receive **adequate medical care** required arising from any adverse event, clinical or laboratory, that may arise during the study. It is good practise for hospital doctors to liaise with a subject's primary care doctor, and the latter should be informed that the subject is involved in a clinical trial.

4. Communication with the ethics committee is a key responsibility of the investigator. This is not limited to applying for permission to undertake the study but also includes maintaining records of the committee's approval of the protocol, consent forms, the recruitment strategy. In addition, a copy of any 'Investigator's Brochure' and annual status reports and a final summary trial report must be submitted to the ethics committee, together with any amendments or updates of key trial documents in an ongoing manner.

5. Protocol deviations/amendments. The investigator is responsible for ensuring that the trial is conducted in full compliance with the agreed protocol. Any changes to the conduct of the study must be formalised via a protocol amendment which should be also agreed with the sponsor, ethics committee and, if appropriate by the regulatory authority. Copies of all changes must be kept and where necessary, new consent forms issued.

6. Drug accountability. It is usual for the investigator to formally delegate responsibility for managing the trial supplies to a pharmacist or nurse. Records must be kept of delivery, storage location, dispensing reconciliation and destruction or return of unused experimental materials. Also, it is expected that appropriate compliance checks are included in patient management.

7. Randomisation/blinding. As most trials involving candidate drugs will be double-blind and often compared with placebo (see Chapter 1), it is important for the investigator to keep secure the code-break envelopes and lists, and to make careful records of any occasion when the code needs to be 'broken'.

8. Informed consent. The investigator is responsible for all matters pertaining to informed consent. This includes either writing or reviewing the information provided to ensure all elements relevant to the study are included (full details were provided in Chapter 2), making amendments to forms as necessary during the study and seeking ethics committee approval for these documents. Also the investigator assumes responsibility for obtaining and documenting the subject's consent. In the event that the subject withdraws from the study, the investigator should make every effort to ascertain the reasons for withdrawal.

9. Record keeping (and data). The investigator needs to complete the study forms (Case Record Forms (CRFs)) legibly and completely, and maintain a record of all original source documents – such as laboratory reports and hospital notes. Any corrections to the originals need to be dated, initialled and explained.

10. Progress reports to the sponsor. The investigator should keep the Sponsor appraised of the progress of the study in terms of numbers of patients enrolled, ongoing, withdrawn or completed. Also the sponsor should be informed if there are any significant changes in trial staff at the study site.

11. Serious adverse events occurring during a drug trial need to be reported to the sponsor immediately and have a written follow-up report prepared detailing the outcome. These events also need to be reported to the appropriate ethics committee. [The sponsor will usually arrange reporting to the relevant regulatory authority.] Frequently, additional reporting requirements will be detailed in the protocol for specific clinical or laboratory abnormalities which may be critical to safety evaluations.

12. Trial termination or suspension. If, for any reason, the trial is suspended or terminated, the investigator should inform all subjects and take care of appropriate therapy and follow-up for them. If the suspension or termination is a decision by the investigator, they should inform the sponsor and provide a written explanation. In all cases, the investigator should inform the institution (where applicable) and the ethics committee.

Ethics Committee and Sponsors' Responsibilities

The bulk of GCP requirements are directed towards the sponsor, requiring these organisations to have thorough professional and standardised procedures for all aspects of clinical conduct. To the extent that these impinge on the researcher in, for example, protocol design and monitoring, they will be described in subsequent chapters. The responsibilities of ethics committees are similarly carefully proscribed, as mentioned in Chapter 4.

CHAPTER 6

PROTOCOLS AND INVESTIGATOR BROCHURES

Clinical Trial Protocols
Investigator Brochure

Clinical Trial Protocols

A clinical trial protocol is a comprehensive document that describes the design and procedures of a trial and forms the basis of agreements between investigators and research funders, and also ethics committees and licensing authorities. This document must provide all necessary guidance for the doctors, nurses, pharmacists, laboratory and all other staff at the study site. It must also provide the sponsor's regulatory, supplies and data management staff, statisticians and trial managers with all the information they require for ensuring resources are available to supply drugs and equipment, design a database, apply appropriate analysis and monitor the trial correctly. Box C includes a list of topics that a protocol must address to comply with ICH GCP.

Most protocols, particularly those destined for multicentre and multinational studies, develop through several drafts as investigators and other experts provide input. It is important that all potential investigators consider the protocol at the earliest stage to ensure that the design, patient selection and procedures are feasible, in general, and for their particular site.

Very often the final protocol contains compromises, particularly from individual clinicians who might feel different measures or comparators or selection criteria would be more appropriate. The research funder may display little flexibility, particularly if there are published guidelines from regulatory authorities. Similarly however, if the researcher knows that local healthcare policy on, for example, referrals or admissions, renders the protocol impractical at their site, it is imperative that these issues are clarified in advance.

Often the sponsor will organise a meeting for all principal investigators/researchers to discuss the design and logistics of the study – or simply to develop and finalise the protocol. Investigator meetings, particularly those to agree multinational protocols, are discussed in Chapter 3.

GCP Protocol Content

Identification (title, date, name and address of sponsor, principal investigator and laboratory).

Background information
- on investigational product (including preclinical and clinical studies, details and justification of drug administration)
- relevant literature to the trial.

Trial objectives.

Trial design
- Description of trial design in text plus schematic diagram of procedures
- Primary and secondary endpoints
- Measures to reduce bias (e.g. randomisation, blinding and procedures for code-breaking)
- Description of treatments (including dosage and packaging/labelling) and accountability procedures
- Duration of subject participation and follow-up
- Data to be recorded on CRFs and source data
- Criteria for subject withdrawal and trial termination
- Subject selection and withdrawal
- Inclusion and exclusion criteria
- How to withdraw subjects – data collection, replacement.

Subject treatment
- Treatment regimes
- Concomitant medication – permitted or disallowed
- Procedures for monitoring subject compliance.

Efficacy assessments
- Efficacy parameters and how they will be assessed, recorded and analysed.

Safety assessments
- Safety parameters
- How they will be assessed, recorded and analysed
- Methods for eliciting, reporting and following-up adverse events.

Statistics
- A description of statistical methods including level of significance
- Number of subjects, total and per centre, and justification for sample size
- Procedures for managing missing data or protocol deviations
- Selection of analyses populations (e.g. all randomised subjects, all available subjects, etc).

Access to source data
- For monitoring, audits, inspections, etc.

Ethics, financing and insurance (financing and insurance may be addressed in a separate agreement).

Data handling and record-keeping.

Publication policy.

Protocols form the basis of a formal agreement with the sponsor or funding body and are subject to a signature confirming that the principal investigator undertakes to comply with the protocol in every particular. Realistically, there are often occasions when research projects do not go according to plan. In this event the investigator is obliged to document any deviations to the agreed protocol and explain why these happened.

Protocol amendments need to be agreed in writing between all parties and submitted for approval to ethics committee (and sometimes to regulatory authorities). Such amendments cause much administrative burden; they may require changes to the CRF, consent forms, database and analysis plans, and are much to be avoided!

The protocol is generally accompanied by extensive appendices that include consent and information forms, and sample CRFs. Depending on the nature of the study, it may also be appropriate to append methods for diagnosis or measurement.

In addition, many sponsors append a list of sponsor and investigator responsibilities and a copy of the latest version of the Declaration of Helsinki and, for multicentre studies, a list of all investigator sites and key staff involved, and contact details of monitors.

Investigator Brochure

So that an investigator can be confident that they are fully informed about an "investigational product(s)" the sponsor should provide, and discuss, an 'investigator brochure' which describes all details of the drug. This document is a mandatory part of GCP and it has been known for auditors to seek confirmation of the researcher's familiarity with its content. It is particularly important, in the management and reporting of adverse events, that the investigator is sufficiently conversant with the pharmacology and previous adverse events associated with the drug, to judge what is unexpected.

The investigator brochure is also made available to the ethics committee and must be kept up to date throughout the clinical development of a new drug. The investigator brochure should be identified by sponsor and drug name and also version number, date approved and reference to any superseded editions, for clarity. The contents of the investigator brochure are laid down in GCP and shown in Box D. This is a highly confidential document and may include a confidentiality agreement to be signed by the investigator.

Contents of Investigator Brochure

D

Summary.

Introduction.

Physical, chemical and pharmaceutical properties and formulation (including storage and handling instructions).

Non-clinical studies (including pharmacology, toxicology, pharmacokinetic and metabolism studies and a discussion of their relevance to humans).

Effects in humans.

Pharmacokinetics and metabolism in man, including population subgroups and drug-drug interactions.

Safety and efficacy, including pharmacodynamics, efficiency and dose response, summaries of ADRs for all clinical trials, precautions or special monitoring required, plus, ideally, a summary of each completed clinical trial. Any marketing experience should be summarised.

Summary of data and Guidance for investigators. (An overall interpretation and discussion of information and implications for future clinical trials, notably adverse event handling.)

CHAPTER 7

MANAGEMENT OF TRIAL SUPPLIES AND DOCUMENTS

Drug Supplies and Accountability
    Open Label Supplies
Equipment for Trial Assessments
Disposables for Biological Samples
Trial Documentation

As the protocol is being developed the requisite supplies for the study become clear. Depending on the type of trial and research setting, these may include:

> Double-blind trial medication

> Equipment for assessments

> Disposables for biological samples

> Trial documentation

If the study is commercially sponsored, the investigator may reasonably expect all supplies to be provided, delivered and explained by R&D department staff, such as a monitor. The investigator is then only responsible for using them correctly and keeping good records. If the study is sponsored by the public or voluntary sector, the investigator will often need to plan, order and account for all the supplies.

Drug Supplies and Drug Accountability

Most clinical trials involving drugs are designed to be double-blind, with the result that medication is prepacked for each (numbered) patient, by a research pharmacy, using a random allocation list. The medication needs to be clearly labelled with the trial and patient identification code, treatment period and instructions for use and storage. The batch/serial number and expiry date should also be provided; this is particularly important in the early stages of development when only short-term stability tests may be completed. Details of the actual treatment allocated to each numbered patient in a double-blind study are kept at the investigational site in individual, sealed 'code-breaker' envelopes. These can be opened in cases of emergency, as described in Chapter 9.

The supplies need to be stored in a secure place under appropriate conditions – in hospital studies this means the pharmacy, but community doctors may need to make special provision to prevent unauthorised use or deterioration of the drug supplies. The management of experimental drugs must be covered by written procedures encompassing delivery, storage, inventory at the site, dispensing and return of unused drugs by each subject, and also return to the sponsor or disposal.

Investigators are required to designate an appropriate person to be responsible for keeping meticulous records of all these aspects of drug supplies; it should be possible to reconcile all experimental supplies. Usually the sponsor will provide a dispensing record; otherwise these must be created to suit the study and record-keeping methods.

If a researcher seeks to conduct a drug trial independent of the manufacturer, s/he can apply to them for double-blind or unmarked supplies, explaining the purpose of the study and providing a comprehensive protocol. If the drug is marketed, the company is likely to be co-operative, but they will review the protocol very carefully and may suggest amendments as a condition to supplying their drugs. If the drug in question is not yet licensed (for that indication) the response is more likely to be negative since such studies should be submitted to the licensing authority and also monitored and audited rigorously to demonstrate GCP compliance. Most companies prefer to develop drugs themselves according to a strategic plan under their control. The preparation of double-blind materials from several sources can be a complex (and expensive) process for an individual doctor to undertake and it may be prudent to enrol the assistance of a specialist drug trial packaging company.

It is important that investigators do not begin dispensing trial medication until the regulatory, ethical and administrative approvals for the study, at that site, have been received. Also, the medication must only be used for patients enrolled in the study according to the protocol.

'Open Label' Supplies

Sometimes an investigator will wish to continue treating a patient openly with an unlicensed drug beyond the formal randomised trial period. (This is particularly tempting when patients suffer from a chronic condition, have experienced substantial benefit from the new treatment and where there are no satisfactory alternatives.) Often such a practice is described in an 'extension protocol' which dictates the circumstances under which continued treatment is acceptable to the regulatory authorities and ethics committees. This option should be discussed in advance as it has implications for the trial and for the patient and doctor involved. Firstly, one must consider when the code should be broken to identify the treatment (in a double-blind study) and whether this was included in the analysis plan. Secondly, an unlicensed drug needs to be subject to careful safety monitoring so both patients and doctors need to be prepared for continued regular review visits and appropriate outcome measures and safety tests as a condition for extension or 'open-label' supplies. Sometimes these patients provide valuable long-term data under relatively 'normal' conditions which is useful for gauging the actual effectiveness of the new drug.

If no extension protocol has been agreed the doctor may contact the manufacturer and request 'named-patient supplies' which are, not surprisingly, provided for individual named patients and carry with them a commitment for the doctor to maintain careful records of dispensing and outcome. Such requests are not always granted because of the burden of administration on the manufacturer – the decision depends on the stage of development, and the nature of the drug and condition being treated.

Equipment for Trial Assessments

It is naturally important that well-established methods of assessment are employed within clinical trials of new interventions. The methodology should be clearly specified in the protocol so that different sites in a multicentre trial can follow the same procedures. Often, specialist equipment will be obtained or employed specifically for the research project. Clearly it is important that any sensitive equipment is stabilised and calibrated before use and any necessary training completed before the trial commences. Also, manufacturers' recommendations should be followed for recalibrating and undertaking reproducibility checks throughout the study to ensure data validity. Where baseline drift and other alterations do occur, researchers should keep careful records so that appropriate adjustments can be made to raw data.

Occasionally, in a multicentre trial, the sponsor will provide standardised equipment to all centres, to minimise measurement differences between sites. The researcher must then be sure that all trial staff familiarise themselves with a new system. Even a new version of a rating scale may take some practice, to avoid a training effect showing in the data analysis.

Disposables for Biological Samples

In community-based studies it is not uncommon for the sponsor to employ a central laboratory or, even themselves, to provide syringes, laboratory tubes, and the like, for collecting and storing biological samples. The researcher needs to be satisfied that all staff involved are aware of the proper procedures for labelling, despatching and storing biological samples, as these may be critical to the outcome of the study. Identification of samples at a later date can often cause problems so it is worth ensuring that freezer-proof labels and pens are used, and each subject's samples are stored discretely.

Trial Documentation

At the beginning of the study the researcher will need a supply of case record forms, consent forms, forms for reporting serious adverse events (SAEs), a code list and also a wide range of reference documents pertinent to the study. Most researchers create and maintain orderly (GCP) study files which contain all the necessary trial documentation from the outset. Tables 1 and 2 list the management documents considered essential under GCP.

It is important to set up the files before the first patient is involved and then to maintain them throughout the project. In particular, it is important to keep the screening and enrolment logs up to date and to familiarise oneself with the documentary procedures for adverse events and emergencies, particularly when code-breaking is involved.

Table 1: Essential documents that should be held by investigators before the clinical phase of the study begins

Document	Investigator should retain
Signed protocol, including amendments	Yes
Sample case report forms	Yes
Patient information and consent form + Advertisement for subject recruitment	Yes
Investigator agreement on final protocol /Financial agreement	Yes
Investigator's brochure	Yes

Local variation on
    Patient information
    Consent form
    Advertising
	Yes

Ethics approval and composition of committee	Yes
Regulatory authority approval/ notification, e.g. CTX	If applicable
Insurance statement	Where required
Investigator's qualifications (CV)	Yes
List of investigators	Yes
Medical/Laboratory technical procedures (certification/accreditation/QC)	Yes
Normal ranges	If applicable
Instructions on handling trial product	Yes
List of pharmacy contacts	If applicable
List of signatures	Yes
Decoding procedures (for blinded trials)	Yes
Pre-trial initiation report (provided by sponsor)	Yes

Maintaining case report forms up to date is also an important, if onerous, task; Chapter 8 provides details of GCP principles with regard to CRF completion and management. In an industry-sponsored drug trial, researchers can expect some assistance with trial documentation from the study monitor, but the same organisation will send auditors to check that all the documentation is correctly maintained.

Table 2: Essential documents that should be held by investigator once the clinical phase of the study has begun

Document	Investigator should retain
Sealed code list (identifying treatment for individual patient numbers)	Yes
Any amendments or revisions to Protocol Case record forms Patient information Case record forms Investigator's brochure	Yes
Ethics approvals necessary for any revision to protocol or consent forms	Yes
Regulatory approvals necessary for any revisions	Yes
Qualifications (CV) for new investigators	Yes
List of signatures of all staff completing CRFs	Yes
Changes to normal ranges	If applicable
Updates of medical/ laboratory procedures	Yes
Records of any drug or trial materials shipment + drug accountability at site, and disposal, if appropriate	Yes
Record of communications: letters, notes on telephone calls & meetings	Yes
Completed CRFs: Includes SAE reports from that site CRF corrections	Yes (Copy)
Source documents	Yes
Signed consent forms	Yes
SAE reports of unexpected and serious adverse events to regulatory authority, sponsor and ethics committee + all related correspondence	Yes
Notification of new safety information from sponsor	Yes
Interim/ Annual reports to ethics committees if required	Yes
Record of stored blood or tissue samples, if any	Yes

On completion of the trial, the final report should be added to the study file of 'essential documents', the location of source documents noted and the entire study file archived securely. These essential documents should be kept at the investigator site for two years after the candidate drug is marketed (or two years after development is cancelled). Access may be requested by monitors, auditors, ethics committee staff or regulatory authority inspectors.

CHAPTER 8

CASE REPORT FORM DESIGN AND MANAGEMENT

Case Report Form Design
Case Report Form Management
Source Data Verification

Case Report Form Design

Case report forms (CRFs) are printed, optical or electronic documents which are designed for recording all of the information required by the protocol, for one trial subject. Occasionally also called case record forms or folders, each set of forms constitutes the most tangible end product of many hours of research.

It is a rare skill to be able to structure the CRF so that it not only includes all the necessary information, but is also easy to complete, unambiguous and convenient for checking and entering onto a computer. Most forms are completed in the presence of a patient in the context of a caring consultation. If they are complex or unclear, the entire project may be compromised. Sponsors are often tempted to produce a form which primarily suits their data management staff. Therefore, it is very important that draft forms are discussed with, and piloted by, the doctors, nurses and technicians who will complete them.

Most CRFs include a selection checklist and a patient history/demography form to be completed at baseline. A medication record, clinical and laboratory assessments, and adverse event forms are repeated for each subsequent visit. An end of study or premature withdrawal form is also included. In addition to those forms completed by the doctor or nurse running the study, the CRF may also include diary cards or self-assessment forms for the patient. Often, the informed consent form and information sheet are packed into the front of the CRF.

Usually the CRF will be printed on NCR (no carbon required) paper, with perforations to facilitate removing copies, and bound into books. Every page should be identified with the trial number, patient number and perhaps a centre number. Most CRFs are designed to be signed and dated on every page.

The experienced CRF designer will incorporate visit dividers and flow charts or aide-memoires into the CRF. A well-designed form should require minimal instructions. Careful thought is also needed to minimise transcription of data (e.g. laboratory tests) as this always introduces errors, and wastes time.

Attention to the site(s) where forms will be completed (e.g. theatre versus consulting room) and consideration of the number of different people involved in providing assessments, may result in improved design. Also, it is very useful if the questions are presented in the order in which the tests or history would normally be undertaken by that researcher or institution.

One of the most common frustrations of research is a printed question offering several options – none of which apply! Usually this is the Not Known/Not Done/Not Applicable option. Another very common problem relates to asking too many (peripheral) questions. This rarely occurs when the forms are designed and completed by the same person! When reviewing draft CRFs one should try to gauge whether a piece of information will be 1) useful and 2) analysed – if not, it is not worth recording! Quite apart from the waste of everyone's time, a burdensome CRF may lead to poorer quality data collection overall, so that the really important results suffer. Also, if too many (for example, laboratory) tests are performed, there is a higher likelihood of chance abnormalities.

Good design is especially important when patients are being asked to collect data. Instructions and questions should be in language appropriate for the lay person, and always available in the patient's native tongue. It should not be assumed that patients, young or old, will necessarily understand how to complete a Visual Analogue Scale or even understand a matrix question laid out in a table. Patients are frequently given diary cards on which to record events, symptoms and medications taken. Ideally these should be sturdily made on card and folded to fit a handbag or wallet. Diary cards should always be numbered and dated before being handed out. The majority of patients are pleased to be involved in this way and may find collecting personal information helpful to understanding their disease and its management, but some may find it burdensome or confusing.

Increasingly, electronic case report forms and scanning of optical forms are being employed in clinical trials. Some of the best innovations are genuinely time-saving for both researchers and data management, and systems where multicentre research data can be entered directly onto computer and transmitted to a central monitoring centre (remote data entry) can be very helpful. However, not all studies lend themselves to this approach and some patients (if not researchers!) can be understandably resistant to conducting every interview via computer screen, particularly if it takes much longer than traditional form completion. Where direct data entry is practised, researchers must be able to print off an individual patient report, to enable review by sponsor monitors and auditors. Also, an electronic CRF should be stored in such a way that the original record cannot be changed without a full audit trail.

Case Report Form Management

Under GCP, researchers are responsible for ensuring the accuracy, completeness and legibility of all the data in the CRFs. All the data in CRFs should be consistent with the source documents, such as patient notes or laboratory printouts. Any discrepancies should be explained in writing and any changes to the original entry of the CRF dated and initialled by authorised staff.

CRFs also need to be completed in a timely manner – it is most unwise to let time elapse after the patient visit before completing the relevant forms. Results from laboratory and other tests generally return later, so time needs to be allocated for their review, together with patients' notes, to ensure 1) all is well and 2) the data are maintained up to date. The importance of this becomes evident if, perhaps, a colleague needs to deal with a serious adverse event for that patient, but also at a more mundane level, the scale of work involved and potential for confusion can increase rapidly in most trials. Creating and maintaining good quality records is one of the least attractive and most onerous of tasks in clinical trials, but the discipline will reduce queries when data are monitored and analysed.

At frequent intervals during a sponsored study, a monitor (sometimes called a Clinical Research Associate or CRA) will visit the investigator to discuss the study progress and review the data. All CRFs should be made available to this monitor, whose job it is to verify the appropriateness of the patient recruitment, the completeness of data collection and the validity of that data against source documents. Usually the same individual will have delivered and explained study forms and procedures to all research staff at the site at the beginning of the study.

The monitor may spend several hours checking the CRFs and noting any queries or anomalies, which are then reviewed, together with the investigator, on site. Hopefully all such queries can be resolved during the visit, although sometimes it will be necessary to check a result with the laboratory or with the patient at the next visit. No CRF originals should be removed from the site until the data are complete and any evident queries resolved and corrected. The investigator always retains a copy of each CRFs at the research site. It is not unusual for further queries to be raised by the sponsor once the data are entered onto a database. Usually the monitor provides a list of these promptly; the investigator then reviews the queries, and provides corrections (including correcting the site copies). Monitors are not permitted to make changes or corrections to the clinical or laboratory results on the CRF.

Source Data Verification

The investigator is responsible not only for completing CRFs correctly but also for maintaining appropriate source documents and ensuring that the two sets of information are fully consistent. Inevitably there is an element of duplication, since CRFs do not usually become part of the patient's case notes, which must also contain key information. Each sponsor company has its own standard operating procedure which will specify that items must be verified by the trial monitor. They are likely to include:

- A statement that the patient is involved in a named study and study number
- Dates of enrolment and subsequent visits, completion or withdrawal from study
- All prescriptions and changes in medication with dates
- Adverse events
- Key efficacy and safety results

Part of the informed consent process serves to obtain permission from patients for sponsor representatives to inspect their medical records. Usually, therefore, the investigator will produce each trial patient's case notes together with the CRFs for the monitor to review at each visit. For long studies in busy hospitals this may prove a burden to medical records staff, in which case it is sensible to agree in advance which patient notes are required at each visit, as source data verification tends only to be performed on two or three occasions per patient. Source data verification may be considered as irksome by some researchers but is now a mandatory aspect of GCP. Sponsor companies are obliged to take seriously any significant discrepancy between source documents and CRFs as they may reduce the validity of the final data. If they have serious concerns about the data quality, a full site audit may be arranged and recruitment could be suspended at that site.

CHAPTER 9

ADVERSE EVENTS IN CLINICAL TRIALS

Adverse Event Reporting

Code-breaking and Emergencies

In the evaluation of any new intervention it is obviously important to establish the balance of risk compared to the potential benefits. Investigators therefore need to have a clear understanding of the importance of identifying, managing and reporting adverse events in clinical trials.

Adverse Event Reporting

Regulations under GCP have much to say about adverse events and provide rules for the information to be collected and reported. An important distinction exists between those adverse events designated serious and those considered non-serious (irrespective of severity).

E

Definitions of Adverse Events

An adverse event is any untoward medical occurrence in a trial subject or patient. It is differentiated from an adverse reaction as no causal relationship needs to be established.

A serious adverse event or drug reaction is any untoward medical occurrence that at any dose:

Results in death

Is life threatening

Requires hospitalisation or prolongation of existing hospitalisation

Results in persistent or significant disability/incapacity

or

Is a congenital anomaly/birth defect.

An unexpected adverse drug reaction is one which is not mentioned in the investigator brochure.

Any serious adverse event needs to be reported immediately to the trial sponsor and then followed up with a written report detailing:

- Patient's trial number
- Gender, Age
- Details of suspected agent – name, batch number, route, dates and doses administered
- Details of other treatments
- Description of events, date and time of onset, severity, setting, duration and outcome.

Sponsors are obliged to report serious and unexpected adverse drug reactions within seven days if they are fatal or life-threatening, or otherwise within 15 days. Sponsors usually provide comprehensive forms, complying with national regulations, on which investigators provide details of adverse events. When researching a new pharmaceutical, it is usual to discuss serious adverse events management with the appropriate clinician (e.g. Head of Pharmacovigilance) within the sponsor company. These doctors should have all the latest available information on the clinical use of the drug and be in a position to advise about appropriate tests to undertake, relevant supportive measures, possible drug-drug interactions, etc. In theory, much of this information should be available in the investigator's brochure, but in practice it is difficult to keep this document constantly updated. However, investigators should ensure that they are fully informed about any trial drug so that they can make appropriate decisions about patient care and judgements about any causal relationship. The 'Summary of Data and Guidance for the Investigator' section of the investigator brochure should prove particularly helpful as it is designed specifically to assist with recognition and treatment of possible overdose and adverse drug reactions, based on previous clinical experience and the pharmacology of the new drug.

Most researchers faithfully report serious events when they occur. More difficult is ensuring that a detailed follow-up report with outcome is compiled in a timely manner. This can easily be overlooked, particularly if the patient recovers swiftly without sequelae, or if they are transferred to another hospital/doctor's care.

Investigators also need to inform their local ethics committee about serious and unexpected adverse drug reactions and in some circumstances, may need to amend consent forms. Sometimes, a protocol will specify that certain non-serious adverse events or laboratory abnormalities are critical to safety evaluations, in which case these need to be reported to the study sponsor accordingly.

In the event of a trial patient or subject dying, a researcher will need to supply the sponsor with additional information such as autopsy reports.

Code-breaking and Emergencies

In the context of a serious adverse event occurring in a double-blind study, it is often desirable to break the trial code to establish which treatment a patient is receiving. This raises a number of issues pertinent to the wellbeing of the individual and the validity of the trial. Firstly, the wellbeing of the patient is paramount so individual sealed envelopes that, when opened, allow the treatment regimen for a particular patient to be identified must be available, and accessible, at the investigator site. If the study is in a hospital setting, often the pharmacy hold the code-breaker envelopes or perhaps they are kept in the departmental office. A community-based study investigator may keep the code-breaker locked in their desk. In either case, the important issue is that, in an emergency, they can be accessed – possibly for Accident and Emergency colleagues. The ID card carried by all patients/subjects in a GCP trial should enable Accident and Emergency staff to contact the researcher or the sponsor, and to break the code if necessary to ascertain the treatment(s) being received.

The protocol should include the procedure for breaking the code for an individual patient. This renders the investigator 'unblinded' for this patient only. Such an action should be reported to the sponsor and documented carefully.

An alternative to investigator-held code-breakers is to employ a Data Monitoring committee. This independent group can be established by the sponsor or by the Trial Steering Committee and its aim is to assess unblinded trial data (progress, safety and critical efficacy) at intervals and to advise whether to continue, modify or stop a trial (see Chapter 11).

CHAPTER 10

REPORTING AND DISSEMINATING RESULTS

Clinical Trial Reports
Disseminating the Results
Systematic Reviews and Meta-analysis

Clinical Trial Reports

Most investigators wish to see the trial data analysed promptly, and an appropriate report produced, once the clinical phase of the trial is complete. In commercially sponsored trials, responsibility for compiling a report rests with the sponsor. However, the principal investigator has a key role in reviewing that report and signing the final version as a true and accurate representation of the completed project.

Most sponsors seek to involve investigators in both the reporting and dissemination of the results of the study. The strategy and agreements for presenting and publishing the results should be discussed and recorded at the protocol stage, to avoid any unseemly debate or misunderstanding at a later date. This is particularly important for multicentre studies, where no single investigator may have the right to publish the entire study results. In some circumstances, the sponsor may be more interested in a report for regulatory purposes than a publication, particularly prior to licensing. However, a paper may be a key motivator for an investigator/researcher and their institution and it should be possible to satisfy both needs in a timely manner. Often the sponsor will organise a post-trial meeting of all investigators to present the results and discuss their interpretation. This provides a good opportunity for investigators to set their own research in context, to hear other perspectives and to question the statistician about the analysis. These meetings usually include further discussion about publications and presentations – to select appropriate journals, authors, meetings and presenters.

Investigators are required to send a summary of the trial report to the institution management and also to the ethics committee. This can be a one-page summary, often prepared by the sponsor for a multicentre trial.

Since clinical trial reports on new medicines are generally used in a submission to regulatory authorities for marketing applications, commercial sponsors will usually produce an integrated clinical and statistical report, acceptable to all regulatory bodies. Such a document is subject to an ICH Guideline (Note for Guidance on Structure and Content of Clinical Study Reports) which was approved in 1995. Each 'clinical study report' is a comprehensive document that includes a list of all participating investigators and their affiliations, role and qualifications. It also describes the administrative structure of the study (e.g. co-ordinating investigator, steering and monitoring committees, and so forth), and investigators' signatures are often required in an appendix.

Once satisfied that the report is correct, the investigator is required to archive it with other essential trial documents, as described in Table 2 in Chapter 7.

Disseminating the Results

Many funders now request dissemination plans together with the original study proposal since there is a danger that funding and enthusiasm may diminish by the reporting stage (as research energies are diverted into the next exciting project!). However tempting, there is an implicit obligation to patients and colleagues to place research in the public domain whenever it might be valuable. Clearly, some early phase drug efficacy and safety studies have limited public interest until there is a prospect of a product licence, so some delay may be appropriate. Recently products launched without published sources of evidence have caused justifiable frustration within the medical profession.

Researchers need to consider the most appropriate means of disseminating trial results and ways to get research findings integrated into practice. This is a particular emphasis in MRC trials but other sponsors, notably NHS and charity funders, also seek to ensure that the outcomes of research are applied. This often proves easier said than done, but if the trial results are generalisable then opportunities to inform medical, nursing and scientific colleagues should be sought. In the UK, the National Research Register and other trial registers not only help avoid unnecessary duplication but also provide a mechanism to inform other researchers. Although papers in peer-reviewed journals and conference presentations may be appropriate, if the results are principally of interest to one institution or community, a more local mechanism should be explored.

Systematic Reviews and Meta-analysis

However well designed and extensive, a single clinical trial rarely provides sufficient evidence to justify changing clinical practice. Individual studies addressing the same research question will often have different patient selection criteria, different definitions of disease and/or measurement techniques. Therefore, reading a number of individual study papers can leave the reader unsure of the 'true' efficacy and safety of a new intervention. Consequently, systematic reviews are now routinely employed to establish whether the results from different trials are consistent and generalisable across populations or care-settings.

Qualitative systematic reviews involve a researcher (often an expert in the field) undertaking a comprehensive search of the literature using a professional search strategy, selecting publications according to a pre-determined set of criteria and integrating the findings in a clear and concise review. Such reviews can be of great value to medical decision-makers, whether as an individual or for setting health policy and formulating guidelines.

Quantitative systematic reviews or meta-analyses can yield increased power, which may be very important when small effects or infrequent events are being assessed. They also permit increased precision of effect.

Although GCP guidelines apply to individual trials, recent ICH guidance on statistical principles for clinical trials urges manufacturers to consider including meta-analyses in the strategic plan, so that common features of design can be identified at the outset of a programme of trials. This is particularly important when using statistical methods to produce a summary and synthesis of the evidence on safety and efficacy, as in the Expert Reports required for EU marketing applications.

Ideally, a meta-analysis should encompass an analysis of all individual patient data across all available studies. This is considered a far superior method than a meta-analysis using aggregate data, due to the increased accuracy and completeness of the subsequent analyses. This process is very time-consuming for the independent researcher but relatively straightforward for a commercial sponsor with its more consistent database.

Where a meta-analysis was not envisaged at the outset of a range of clinical trials, the heterogeneity may present as a tension between methodological differences which render trials incompatible on the one hand, and the desire to include all studies, on the other. Selectively excluding a number of studies on the basis that they were poorly designed may lead to criticism that the analysis is not objective, whilst including badly designed studies may confound the outcome and result in 'adding apples and pears'. Meta-analysis therefore has its detractors, and in certain circumstances, is neither advisable or possible.

CHAPTER 11

TRIAL MANAGEMENT AND AUDIT

Trial Steering Committees
Data Monitoring Committees
Investigator Standard Operating Procedures
Sponsor Monitoring
Inspections and Audits
   GCP Inspections
   Sponsor Audits

Good Clinical Practice describes two forms of trial monitoring – that organised to monitor progress and compliance with the protocol and GCP guidelines, and that arranged to review safety and efficacy data (usually at preset intervals) to protect the wellbeing of subjects. Where the sponsor is the Medical Research Council, an independent steering committee is elected to assume the former role.

Trial Steering Committees

The Medical Research Council encourages all investigators to avail themselves of expert advice independent of themselves and their institution. This will normally be in the form of a 'Trial Steering Committee' (TSC) and a 'Data Monitoring (and ethics) Committee', depending on the nature of the trial. It is suggested that the TSC consists of an independent chairman, a couple of others, plus one or two senior investigators. Statisticians and co-ordinators, and observers from the host institution and the MRC should be invited to meetings, which initially are used to approve the protocol and consent form before applying for funding. Thereafter meetings should be scheduled at least annually. Either the principal investigator or the funder (e.g. MRC) may call for and organise these meetings, which should be accurately minuted.

The role of the TSC is to supervise the study with respect to protocol adherence, progress and patient safety, including review of new information. The direct management of the study remains the responsibility of the investigator. Clear targets for patient recruitment and data collection should be agreed with the investigators in advance and reviewed at each meeting, including attrition rates, serious adverse events and any actions needed.

If investigators experience delays and apply for extensions to grants, the funders may require evidence from the TSC that every effort has been made to achieve the targets originally agreed. At the end of the study, the TSC also has a role in ensuring the results are disseminated appropriately.

Data Monitoring Committees

Both ICH principles and MRC guidelines for GCP suggest that investigators should obtain expert input from an independent data monitoring committee. Ideally this group should be small (3-4 members), include both an expert clinician in the field and a medical statistician, and operate according to written procedures. Its role is to review the data, unblinded if necessary, to protect the rights and wellbeing of the patients. The committee assesses the progress of the clinical trial, including the safety data and critical efficacy endpoints at specified intervals, and recommends to the sponsor or trial steering committee (MRC funded trials) whether to continue, modify or stop a trial. It is important that no-one directly involved with the study should have access to unblinded data. Such a committee will not be appropriate for all studies or all interventions, but there are many occasions where this type of objectivity can greatly benefit a research programme.

Investigator Standard Operating Procedures

Research sponsors are required under GCP to produce detailed SOPs for all aspects of clinical research, which have proved useful for clarifying and standardising processes, training staff and apply quality assurance. Some research institutions and clinics have also found it helpful to develop or adapt written procedures for routine trial-related activities, such as document handling and storage, obtaining consent, randomisation and dispensing. These may also incorporate nursing and clinical protocols.

Specimen SOPs for researchers, including checklists, have recently been published, suitable for adapting to different institutions (see Further Reading). Investigator SOPs are not currently a requirement under GCP.

Sponsor Monitoring

Under GCP, the investigator agrees that the site will be monitored by the sponsor. This task is usually performed by a CRA or monitor working for the manufacturing company or a Contract Research Organisation. The monitor should be adequately qualified, usually with a scientific or medical degree, and trained in clinical trial methodology. They should have a thorough knowledge of the drug or device being studied, the protocol, GCP and those regulatory requirements relevant to the study. Monitors work according to the sponsor's Standard Operating Procedures which encompass issues such as selection of investigators, initiating the trial, supplies accountability and monitoring visits.

During the evaluation of facilities, as described in Chapter 3, the sponsor will discuss the extent of monitoring for an individual study and determine the appropriate intensity/frequency of monitoring.

The study initiation meeting is an important opportunity to review all the key documentation and supplies for the trial, the logistics of all the measurements, the recruitment strategy, the allocation of patients to treatment and CRF completion. It also provides an opportunity for all the investigational site staff with any involvement in the study to receive an overview of the investigator brochure and protocol, and to establish lines of communication. At this meeting also, the key agreements between Sponsor and investigator concerning the protocol and financial arrangements will be signed and exchanged.

A good monitor can be a great source of information and encouragement to the investigator. Their job is to support and assist the trial (and provide a direct communication link with the sponsor) as well as to review progress. Well in advance of a meeting, they should confirm in writing the schedule, the documents they wish to review and any necessary preparation.

It is not unusual for monitors to have an extensive agenda for each scheduled meeting at an investigator site – see Box F.

Routine Monitoring Visit : Review Topics   **F**

Patient numbers: screening, recruitment, completion, attrition.
Protocol adherence in patient selection.
Informed consent process/records and trial register.
All CRF entries (and accompanying data) since last visit.
Source data verification.
Protocol compliance during follow-up.
Drugs storage, dispensing and accounting records.
Trial Master File (essential documents).
Serious adverse event: reports and follow-up.
GCP compliance.
New information: on drug, study or site.
Problems: logistic or scientific, and agreed actions.

The investigator can do much to reduce the workload of monitoring visits (sometimes lasting one day every month) by collecting together the CRFs, source data and trial master file in advance, and ensuring all are reviewed, signed and up to date.

These regular meetings ought to be mutually useful, so investigators should consider what information or agreement they need, too. The monitor needs a separate room (or at least a quiet corner!) where they can first review all the data before meeting with the investigator(s) to discuss the study. Monitoring is not limited to meetings; monitors will regularly be in touch with investigators by letter and telephone in-between visits, to ascertain patient numbers and discuss any problems or adverse events.

Once the study is complete, the monitor will conduct an 'end of study' or 'closure' meeting at which all outstanding data queries are resolved, unused trial supplies are removed and arrangements made for archiving essential documents. If appropriate, another later meeting may occur to discuss the analysis, report and publication plans.

When an inspection by a regulatory authority or sponsor QA department is announced, the monitor will usually be on-hand to assist the investigator to prepare site documents and explain the processes.

Inspections and Audits

Not every trial site for every study receives an audit from the sponsor or regulatory authority, but it is always a possibility, particularly for the principal centres in important trials. Audits are performed either as part of a strategic plan, with sites in multicentre trials often selected on the basis of statistical sampling, or because either the sponsor or regulatory agency has specifically requested a particular study or site audit. The MRC, as a major sponsor of clinical trials, also has an audit programme and employs QA staff to conduct audits on randomly selected trials. Reports of MRC audits are provided to the investigators for their comments and then passed to the TSC and MRC Board.

GCP Inspections

National agencies are required by ICH GCP to administer a mutually recognised compliance programme with respect to

GCP. This is a form of Quality Assurance and investigators and their institutions must give their agreement, and co-operation, to inspectors either from the national agency or from overseas. Inspectors will not arrive unannounced, but the period of notice can be limited to a few weeks and investigators are expected to make themselves and their records available. The inspection usually consists of an initial meeting of all parties, a period of review while inspectors check the essential documents, and compare CRFs with source documents, and a final meeting at which the outcome and any deficiencies are discussed.

Sponsor Audits

Most sponsor companies will have their own QA department with auditors visiting sites all over the world, while some employ freelance auditors to audit their sites according to sponsor SOPs. In either case, the investigator may expect the sponsor company to agree a mutually convenient date for any audit visit, and for the auditors to be familiar not only with the monitoring processes but also the trial and study drug. The study monitor will be able to explain exactly what is needed and how the audit will be conducted, this is usually very similar to the regulatory authority inspection. The investigator needs to be aware that audits involve additional preparation work and a willingness to be available to answer questions about any aspect of the trial conduct or data collection at that site.

If deficiencies are reported, either via monitoring or an audit, steps should be taken by the investigator to rectify the issue, if possible, or at least to document the reason for the problem and how it will be avoided in future.

In the event of persistent non-compliance with the protocol or GCP, the sponsor is likely to terminate the investigator/site's involvement in the study. Particular concerns include poor management and recording of adverse events, any breach of proper informed consent or major inconsistencies between CRFs and source data.

CHAPTER 12

LABORATORIES AND GOOD LABORATORY PRACTICE

Pre-trial Inspections by Research Sponsors
Introduction to Good Laboratory Practice
Study Management
    Archiving
    Standard Operating Procedures
    Facilities and Systems
    Computer Systems
Responsibilities of Laboratory Personnel
QA Programme and Compliance Monitoring

It is becoming normal practice for those working in a laboratory involved in clinical trials to be subject to various 'inspections' from the sponsor organisation. The aim is for the sponsor to satisfy themselves that the laboratory has not only the expertise and facilities needed, but also the systems to assure the validity of its data. Such inspections usually occur in the context of a discussion on the study plan/protocol of the proposed research project.

Pre-trial Inspections by Research Sponsors

The scope of most pre-trial inspections conducted by sponsors are encompassed in the list of questions in Box G, although there may also be trial specific topics to review.

Pre-trial Laboratory Inspection: Review Topics and Questions   **G**

Number of staff and contact person for the study.
Staff CVs and training records; available and up to date.
Experience in similar research (microbiology/clinical chemistry, data management).
Facilities for sample receipt, testing, storage.
Systems for monitoring identity of samples.
Comprehensive SOPs and evidence of QC system.
Involvement in relevant QA rings.
National laboratory accreditation (e.g. NAMAS, GLP).
Normal ranges (appropriate age and sex) available.
Methodologies (for all measures) available.
Evidence of adequate review of results by an expert.
Evidence that equipment is regularly maintained/calibrated.
Details of computer system and data transfer capacity.
Arrangements for back-up in event of computer/test equipment/electrical failure.
Adequate systems for archiving and retrieving study results.

Some sponsors will also wish to explore matters such as confidentiality, results and status reporting and contractual issues.

Introduction to Good Laboratory Practice

Since it is routine for laboratory tests to be conducted for safety and efficacy evaluations, within clinical trials, it is considered important that the laboratory data are also subject to various quality controls. For those sites involved in the laboratory aspects of clinical research, it is therefore useful to be familiar with the principles of Good Laboratory Practice (GLP).

> "Good Laboratory Practice is a quality system concerned with the organisational process and conditions under which non-clinical health and environmental safety studies are planned, performed, monitored, recorded, archived and reported."

The OECD GLP principles were first introduced in the 1970s, following on from FDA regulations, and were most recently updated and published in 1998 (contact details for obtaining the full text can be found in the appendix). Through the systems for monitoring compliance of GLP, mutual recognition of data generated under GLP amongst OECD member countries is achievable.

Although GLP compliance is not mandatory for clinical studies, increasingly sponsors are requesting adherence as a prerequisite to involvement in major research programmes. This is especially so for pivotal studies to be used in the registration of new drugs, where accurate laboratory tests are an integral part of the efficacy and safety evidence submitted. GLP applies not only to safety monitoring, such as haematology and biochemistry tests, but also to critical test substance assays and other laboratory measures. It also includes guidance on the use of computer systems in research being included in regulatory submissions.

GLP can be divided, for convenience, into three main topics – the management of facilities and studies, the responsibilities of laboratory personnel and the QA and compliance monitoring programmes.

Study Management

For each study, a plan should be produced and approved by the study director, facility management and sponsor. The study plan is a document which defines the objectives, design and conduct of the study, together with any amendments. It can be equated to a laboratory protocol. Box H summarises the content of a GLP Study Plan.

GLP Study Plan   **H**

Study ID: title, purpose, test item and reference item(s) to be used.

Facility and sponsor ID: name and addresses of sponsor, test site and study director and, if appropriate, principal investigator.

Dates: schedule for start and completion, and approval dates.

Test methods.

Design features: justification for test system, full description of test system (e.g. animal species), dosing: level, route, frequency, experimental design: procedures, materials and methods, observations and analyses.

A list of records to be retained.

The study plan is the central document for the GLP study and the study should be conducted in full accordance with it. Each study must have a unique ID, to be employed on all samples and data records.

Data entry should be prompt, accurate and legible and each entry signed and dated. Any changes made subsequently should include a reason for the change and be dated and signed/initialled. Computerised system design should permit full audit trails to show changes.

On completion, a report should be prepared for each study and approved by the study director. In addition to the information listed for the study plan (in Box H), the report should include a summary of the results together with a discussion and conclusions. A QA programme statement and storage location details should also be included.

Archiving

The following documents should be archived (and retained as specified by national authorities):

GLP Archive Contents   **I**

Study Plan

Raw data

Samples of test material* and reference items

Specimens

Final report

QA programme inspection records

CVs, training records and job descriptions of all staff

Records of maintenance and calibration of equipment

Validation documents for the computer systems

SOPs – historical file

         * only as long as evaluable

Archives should be secure, with restricted access. Movement of files in and out should be recorded. The archive should be indexed for rapid retrieval. In the event of a laboratory facility closing, the study archive should be transferred to the research sponsor.

Standard Operating Procedures

A laboratory should have written SOPs, approved by senior management, which are relevant to the activities being performed. The scope of SOPs should include (but are not limited to):

- Test and reference materials: receipt, ID, labelling, handling, sampling and storage.

- Apparatus, materials and reagents: apparatus use, maintenance cleaning and calibration, materials preparation and labelling.

- Computer systems: validation, operation, maintenance, security, change control and back-up.

- Record keeping, reporting, storage and retrieval.

- Test systems (as appropriate): preparation, procedures, observations, specimens, etc.

- QA procedures: planning, performing and reporting inspections.

Published textbooks and manuals can be used as supplements to SOPs. Deviations to laboratory SOPs should be documented by the study director, or site investigator, as applicable.

Facilities and Systems

GLP principles encompass many common sense provisions concerning the adequacy of laboratory premises to undertake specific research studies. These are described in considerable detail in the guidelines but the main points are summarised below.

Facilities need to be of a suitable size and location to meet the requirements of the study and should be designed to permit an adequate degree of separation for the different activities, and also for the storage of supplies, equipment and hazardous substances. In particular, there should be separate areas or rooms for receipt and storage of test items and mixing with vehicles etc, to prevent deterioration or contamination. Archive facilities for documents and specimens need to be secure and protect the contents from deterioration. Waste disposal should be conducted in such a way as to protect the integrity of the studies. Apparatus should be regularly inspected, cleaned, maintained and calibrated according to SOPs, and chemicals should be labelled with ID, expiry date and storage instructions. Receipt and usage of test and reference materials and details of batch numbers and other characteristics should be kept. Samples, for analytical purposes, should be retained for most studies. Where animals and plants are employed in studies, there are specific regulations for their care and record-keeping (see details in published Principles of GLP).

Computer Systems

Since most laboratories now make extensive use of computer systems for data capture, processing and storage, GLP includes guidance for these systems in regulatory trials, and computers used in a laboratory will be reviewed during an inspection. Laboratories therefore need to ensure that the computers are suitable for their intended purpose, and to develop systems and keep documentation with reference to:

Hardware/software	system ID and hardware components
	software components and operating system
	functions performed by software
	overview of data type and flow
	communication links to equipment and other systems
Communication network	including protection from corruption
Control procedures	development documentation
	acceptance testing
	quality control
	documentation of modifications
User manual	authorisation of changes should be included
	staff training should be documented
Security	access should be defined in SOPs
Data	raw data must be retained unchanged
	full audit trails are needed for any changes to original data
	electronic archiving must have facilities to ensure the integrity of the data

Detailed information on the application of GLP principles to computer systems can be found in GLP Advisory Leaflet No 1 from the Department of Health (see Appendix for details).

Responsibilities of Laboratory Personnel

In addition to the overall management of the laboratory facilities (covered in the last section), GLP defines specific roles and responsibilities for a Study Director, a Principal Investigator (for multicentre studies), and other study personnel.

The study director is responsible for the overall conduct of the study and for its final report. Their particular responsibilities are summarised in Box J. The principal investigator is an individual within a multi-site study who takes responsibility for conducting their part of the study in accordance with GLP, as applicable.

Study Director's Responsibilities

J

Approve study plan and amendments by dated signature.

Ensure QA staff have study plan and amendments, and communicate with them throughout study in timely manner.

Ensure study personnel have access to study plan, amendments and SOPs.

In the case of a multi-site study, ensure study plan and report includes identity and definition of the role of a PI, and any other test sites.

Ensure procedures specified in study plan and SOPs are followed; in the event of any deviations, document and take corrective action.

Ensure all raw data generated are fully documented and recorded.

Ensure any computerised systems have been validated.

Sign and date final report to indicate acceptance of responsibility for data validity and extent of compliance to GLP.

On completion, ensure study plan, final report and raw data are archived.

All study personnel should possess a knowledge of GLP applicable to their involvement, should have access to the study plan and SOPs, should follow the instructions provided and should record raw data promptly and accurately. In addition, study personnel are responsible for taking appropriate health and safety precautions so as to minimise risk and ensure the integrity of the study.

QA Programme and Compliance Monitoring

Each laboratory is expected to have a QA programme to assure that individual studies are carried out in accordance with GLP. QA staff should be familiar with the test procedures but not involved in the study, and directly responsible to senior management.

QA staff are responsible for monitoring copies of all study plans and SOPs, and should check that each study plan is compliant with GLP. They also conduct three types of inspections: study; facility; process, as laid down in the inspection SOPs. These inspections are formally reported to senior management and the study director and a formal statement specifying inspections, dates and outcome is prepared. QA staff also review each study report to confirm that methods are accurately described and results reflect the raw data.

In most countries a GLP compliance programme has been established which undertakes regular monitoring of laboratories by inspection, usually every two years, and also study audits at the request of a regulatory authority.

APPENDICES

Further Reading and References

Barker DJP, Rose G. Epidemiology in Medical Practice (Fourth Edition), 1990, Churchill Livingstone.

Bowling A. Research Methods in Health: Investigating Health and Health Services, 1997, Open University Press.

Chalmers I, Altman DG (Eds). Systematic Reviews, 1995, BMJ Publishing Group.

Clinical Standards Advisory Group. Report on Clinical Effectiveness: using stroke care as an example, 1998, HMSO.

Crombie IK, Davies HTO. Research in Health Care: Design, Conduct and Interpretation of Health Services Research, 1996, John Wiley & Sons Ltd.

Crombie IK & Florey CduV. The Pocket Guide to Grant Applications, 1998, BMJ Books.

Daly J, McDonald I, Willis E (Eds). Researching Health Care: Designs, Dilemmas, Disciplines, 1992, Routledge.

Jefferson T, Demicheli V, Mugford M. Elementary Economic Evaluation in Health Care, 1996, BMJ Publishing Group.

Kolman J, Meng P, Scott G. Good Clinical Practice: Standard Operating Procedures for Clinical Researchers, 1998, John Wiley & Son Ltd.

Medical Research Council. MRC Guidelines for Good Clinical Practice in Clinical Trials, 1998, MRC.

O'Donnell, M. Our Oath is Hypocritical. Monitor Weekly, 1995, Mar 1, 44.

Zelen M A New Design for Randomized Clinical Trials. The New England Journal of Medicine, 1979 Vol 300, No 22, pp1242-1246.

ICH and OECD Documents

ICH Topic E3, Note for Guidance on Structure and Content of Clinical Study Reports (CPMP/ICH/137/95), 1995.

ICH Topic E6, Note for Guidance on Good Clinical Practice (CPMP/ICH/135/95), 1996.

ICH Topic E8. Note for Guidance on General Considerations for Clinical Trials (CPMP/ICH/291/95), 1997.

ICH Topic E9, Note for Guidance on Statistical Principles for Clinical Trials (CPMP/ICH/363/96), 1998.

OECD Principles of Good Laboratory Practice (as revised in 1997), 1998, Paris.

Good Laboratory Practice: Advisory Leaflet Number 1: The Application of GLP Principles to Computer Systems, 1995, Department of Health.

Glossary

The following are a selection of definitions derived from ICH GCP documents, together with some commonly used abbreviations

Adverse Event (AE)
Any untoward medical occurrence in a patient or clinical investigation subject administered a pharmaceutical product and which does not necessarily have a causal relationship with this treatment. An adverse event (AE) can therefore be any unfavourable and unintended sign (including an abnormal laboratory finding), symptom, or disease temporally associated with the use of a medicinal (investigational) product, whether or not related to the medicinal (investigational) product.

Audit
A systematic and independent examination of trial related activities and documents to determine whether the evaluated trial related activities were conducted, and the data were recorded, analyzed and accurately reported according to the protocol, sponsor's standard operating procedures (SOPs), Good Clinical Practice (GCP), and the applicable regulatory requirement(s).

Audit Trail
Documentation that allows reconstruction of the course of events.

Compliance (in relation to trials)
Adherence to all the trial-related requirements, Good Clinical Practice (GCP) requirements, and the applicable regulatory requirements.

Confidentiality
Prevention of disclosure, to other than authorized individuals, of a sponsor's proprietary information or of a subject's identity.

Coordinating Investigator
An investigator assigned the responsibility for the coordination of investigators at different centres participating in a multicentre trial.

Contract Research Organization (CRO)
A person or an organization (commercial, academic, or other) contracted by the sponsor to perform one or more of a sponsor's trial-related duties and functions.

Direct Access

Permission to examine, analyze, verify, and reproduce any records and reports that are important to evaluation of a clinical trial. Any party (e.g., domestic and foreign regulatory authorities, sponsor's monitors and auditors) with direct access should take all reasonable precautions within the constraints of the applicable regulatory requirement(s) to maintain the confidentiality of subjects' identities and sponsor's proprietary information.

Essential Documents

Documents which individually and collectively permit evaluation of the conduct of a study and the quality of the data produced.

Good Clinical Practice (GCP)

A standard for design, conduct, performance, monitoring, auditing, recording, analyses and reporting of clinical trials that provides assurance that the data and reported results are credible and accurate and that the rights, integrity and confidentiality of trial subjects are protected.

Independent Data-Monitoring Committee (IDMC) (Data and Safety Monitoring Board, Monitoring Committee, Data Monitoring Committee)

An independent data-monitoring committee that may be established by the sponsor to assess at intervals the progress of a clinical trial, the safety data, and the critical efficacy endpoints, and to recommend to the sponsor whether to continue, modify, or stop a trial.

Impartial Witness

A person, who is independent of the trial, who cannot be unfairly influenced by people involved with the trial, who attends the informed consent process if the subject or the subject's legally acceptable representative cannot read, and who reads the informed consent form and any other written information supplied to the subject.

Informed Consent

A process by which a subject voluntarily confirms his or her willingness to participate in a particular trial, after having been informed of all aspects of the trial that are relevant to the subject's decision to participate. Informed consent is documented by means of a written, signed and dated informed consent form.

Inspection
The act by a regulatory authority(ies) of conducting an official review of documents, facilities, records, and any other resources that are deemed by the authority(ies) to be related to the clinical trial and that may be located at the site of the trial, at the sponsor's and/or contract research organization's (CRO's) facilities, or at other establishments deemed appropriate by the regulatory authority(ies).

International Conference on Harmonisation (ICH)
The objective of the International Conference on Harmonisation is to provide unified standards for the EU, Japan and US to facilitate mutual acceptance of clinical data by regulatory authorities.

Investigator
A person responsible for the conduct of the clinical trial at a trial site. If a trial is conducted by a team of individuals at a trial site, the investigator is the responsible leader of the team and may be called the principal investigator. See also Subinvestigator.

Investigator's Brochure
A compilation of the clinical and non-clinical data on the investigational product(s) which is relevant to the study of the investigational product(s) in human subjects.

Protocol
A document that describes the objective(s), design, methodology, statistical considerations and organisation of a trial.

Regulatory Authorities
Bodies having the power to regulate. In the ICH GCP guideline the expression Regulatory Authorities includes the authorities that review submitted clinical data and those that conduct inspections. These bodies are sometimes referred to as competent authorities.

Serious Adverse Event (SAE) or Serious Adverse Drug Reaction (Serious ADR)
Any untoward medical occurrence that at any dose:
Results in death
Is life-threatening
Requires inpatient hospitalization or prolongation of existing hospitalization
Results in persistent or significant disability/incapacity
Or
Is a congenital anomaly/birth defect

Source Data

All information in original records and certified copies of original records of clinical findings, observations, or other activities in a clinical trial necessary for the reconstruction and evaluation of the trial. Source data are contained in source documents (original records or certified copies).

Source Documents

Original documents, data, and records (e.g., hospital records, clinical and office charts, laboratory notes, memoranda, subjects' diaries or evaluation checklists, pharmacy dispensing records, recorded data from automated instruments, copies or transcriptions certified after verification as being accurate copies, microfiches, photographic negatives, microfilm or magnetic media, x-rays, subject files, and records kept at the pharmacy, at the laboratories and at medico-technical departments involved in the clinical trial).

Sponsor

An individual, company, institution, or organization which takes responsibility for the initiation, management, and/or financing of a clinical trial.

Standard Operating Procedure

Detailed, written instructions to achieve uniformity of the performance of a specific function.

Subinvestigator

Any individual member of the clinical trial team designated and supervised by the investigator at a trial site to perform critical trial-related procedures and/or to make important trial-related decisions (e.g., associates, residents, research fellows). See also Investigator.

Unexpected Adverse Drug Reaction

An adverse reaction, the nature or severity of which is not consistent with the applicable product information (e.g., Investigator's Brochure for an unapproved investigational product or package insert/summary of product characteristics for an approved product) (see the ICH Guidelines for Clinical Safety Data Management: Definitions and Standards for Expedited Reporting).

Abbreviations

ADR	Adverse Drug Reaction
CRA	Clinical Research Associate
CRF	Case Report Form
CRO	Contract Research Organisation
CTC	Clinical Trial Certificate
CTX	Exemption from Clinical Trial Certificate
CV	Curriculum Vitae
EMEA	European Medicines Evaluation Agency
FDA	Food and Drug Administration
GCP	Good Clinical Practice
GLP	Good Laboratory Practice
ICH	International Conference on Harmonisation
ID	Identification (Patient)
IEC	Independent Ethics Committee
IRB	Institutional Review Board
LREC	Local Research Ethics Committee
MCA	Medicines Control Agency
MRC	Medical Research Council
MREC	Multicentre Research Ethics Committee
NHS	National Health Service
OECD	Organisation for Economic Co-operation and Development
QA	Quality Assurance
R&D	Research and Development
RCT	Randomised Clinical Trial
SAE	Serious Adverse Event
SOP	Standard Operating Procedures
SSC	Study Site Co-ordinator

Useful Contacts

AMRC (The Association of Medical Research Charities)
29-35 Farringdon Road
London EC1M 3JB
Tel: 0171 404 6454 / Fax: 0171 404 6448
Email: amrc@mailbox.ulcc.ac.uk
Web: http://www.amrc.org.uk/homepage.htm

ABPI (Association of the British Pharmaceutical Industry)
12 Whitehall, London SW1A 2DY
Tel: 0171-930-3477

ACRPI (The Association of Clinical Research for the
Pharmaceutical Industry)
PO Box 1208
Maidenhead
Berks SL6 3GD
Tel: 01628 829900 / Fax: 01628 829922
Email: acrpi@compuserve.com

ICH Secretariat (International Conference on Harmonisation)
C/o IFPMA
30 rue de St.Jean
PO Box 9, 1211
Geneva 18
Switzerland
Tel: 00 41 22 340 1200

MCA (Medicines Control Agency) GCP Compliance Unit
Room 621A
Market Towers
1 Nine Elms Lane
London SW8 5NQ
Tel: 0171 273 0722 / Fax: 0171 273 0676

MRC (Medical Research Council)
20 Park Crescent
London W1N 4AL
Tel: 0171 636 5422 / Fax: 0171 436 6179

MREC (Multi-Centre Research Ethics Committees)
Sandra Holley
Administrator
South Thames MREC (Enquiries)
Centre of Medical Law and Ethics
King's College, London
Strand
London WC2R 2LS
Tel/Fax: 01323 638613
http://dspace.dial.pipex.com/mrec.

NHS Health Technology Assessment Programme
HTA Programme Manager
Research and Development Directorate
NHS Executive
Room GW52, Quarry House
Quarry Hill
Leeds LS2 7UE
Tel: 0113 254 6194 / Fax: 0113 254 6174/6197
Web: http://www.soton.ac.uk/~wi/ta

NHS Research and Development Directorate
NHS Executive Headquarters
Department of Health
Richmond House
79 Whitehall
London SW1A 2NS
Tel: 0171 210 5556 / Fax: 0171 210 5868
Web: (NHS National R&D Information)
http://libsun.1.jr2.ox.ac.uk:80/nhserdd/national.htm
Web: (NHS National Priority Research Programmes)
http://libsun1.jr2.ox.ac.uk:80/nhserdd/aordd/overview/commr&d.htm

RCGP (Royal College of General Practitioners)
14 Princes Gate
Hyde Park
London SW7 1PU
Tel: 0171 581 3232 / Fax: 0171 225 3047
Email: info@rcgp/org.uk
Web: http://www.rcgp.org.uk

Scottish Office Department of Health
Chief Scientist Office
St Andrew's House
Edinburgh EH1 3DG
Tel: 0131 244 2244 / Fax: 0131 244 2683

Wisdom Schemes Search (Wellcome Trust)
Web: http://wisdom.wellcome.ac.uk/wisdom/schemes/html

Consider it Pure Joy •••

Ann Raven
Third Edition. 1997. 84 pages.
£9.50. ISBN 951739611

Consider It Pure Joy ••• provides a simple introduction to the process of clinical drug development. It demystifies the way in which new medicines are discovered, tested and regulated. This book is intended for those who wish to understand the background to clinical trials from a pharmaceutical company perspective. It provides invaluable information for clinical trials supplies technicians and pharmacists, data management staff, information officers and medical secretaries. **Consider It Pure Joy •••** has now been thoroughly updated and extended.

CONTENTS:
- Drug development ▪ Regulation of drug research
- Good clinical practice ▪ Clinical Investigators
- Trial design and protocols ▪ Case record forms
- Trial supplies ▪ Clinical research associates
- Monitoring and adverse events ▪ Analysis and reports
- Standard operating procedures, audits and archives
- Pharmaco-economics

"The clear and concise writing style makes each page easy to follow and easy to digest ... I would encourage readers to buy copies for their departments so that new clinical staff could be well briefed and sure to start off on the right footing."

JOURNAL OF PHARMACEUTICAL MEDICINE
on the First Edition

ABOUT ACTION HEALTH

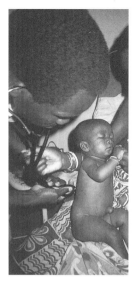

ACTION HEALTH is an International Development Charity based in Cambridge. It was founded in 1984 by a group of health professionals from Britain, India and Africa who had worked overseas with marginalised or isolated communities.

Concerned about the inadequate provision of primary health care and the lack of appropriate training opportunities, this group created **ACTION HEALTH** – an organisation dedicated to enabling communities to establish and strengthen their own health programmes.

ACTION HEALTH works with Non-Governmental Organisations and Ministries of Health in India, Uganda and Tanzania. Recruitment of Health Professionals to work with our partners overseas currently takes place in the UK, and draws on the skills of Health Promotion Specialists, Midwives, Health Visitors, General Practitioners, Occupational Therapists, Physiotherapists and Speech and Language Therapists.

We achieve our goals by:

 experienced professional people to share health and development skills with our overseas partners and their staff.

 networks between overseas partners and other agencies to encourage the sharing of skills, ideas and experiences.

 overseas partners in project planning, implementation, and evaluation.

Achievements in 1997/98

In 1997 **ACTION HEALTH** trebled the number of Ugandan Occupational Therapists who can provide rehabilitative care to the country's two million disabled people. Locally trained Occupational Therapists now number 13.

In Bangalore, India we set up two Well women clinics with a local Non Governmental Organisation to provide sexual health care, education and counselling for women from the slum areas. Previously these services simply did not exist. We trained 21 local women in primary health care, covering a total population of over 44,000 people.

We are the only British health charity working in North Pemba, Tanzania. We have trained local staff in five primary health care units providing health care services to over 50 villages, a population of 50,000.

Long term solutions

When we leave we want the results to last.

We work with local people until they are self-reliant. To date we have been able to withdraw from nearly 60 communities, leaving behind skilled and confident health workers who are able to provide care to thousands of people – and train others for future generations.

ACTION HEALTH VALUES

We believe

- people really can make changes for the better
- no one should suffer unnecessarily from ill health and preventable diseases
- we should enable people to develop long term solutions to problems
- sharing skills and knowledge will develop self-reliance and bring lasting benefits

Cost effective

For every £1 you donate, Action Health spends 87p on direct charitable costs. Voluntary help from returned trainers and office volunteers, low overheads and our commitment to this work keep our costs to a minimum. This ensures that your support is used as effectively as possible.

To continue and expand our programmes in India and Africa we rely on the support of charitable donations. Two-thirds of our funding is currently provided by the Department for International Development, the European Commission, Trusts and Foundations. The rest comes from membership, individuals, companies and community groups.

£20 will enable an **ACTION HEALTH** Trainer to reach local health workers in remote clinics in the poorest parts of Pemba island, Tanzania.

£50 will train a local woman in nursing skills, providing care to 15,000 marginalised tribal people in the hills of Southern India.

£100 will provide a year's training for a local Occupational Therapist in Uganda.

£250 will provide services for testing, counselling and preventative education about STD's and HIV/AIDS for women living in city slums.

Take Action Today!

Membership of **ACTION HEALTH** will entitle you to a copy of our Newsletter and Annual Review and updated information on forthcoming events.

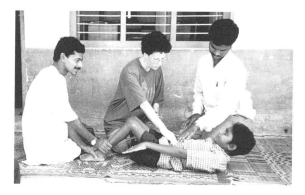

If you are interested in becoming a member or for further information on Action Health contact:

ACTION HEALTH
25 Gwydir Street,
Cambridge
CB1 2LG
Tel: 01223 460853

Order Form

Please send me

Quantity		Value/£
.... copies	@ £10.50 each	....
10% Discount for 20 copies		....
Postage and Packing @ £1 per copy		....
	TOTAL	

Orders should be accompanied by cheques made payable to "**Cambridge Healthcare Research**".

Name and address for despatch:

....

....

....

....

.... Post Code...........................

Cambridge Healthcare Research,
Publications Division,
The Old Institute, High Street, Coton,
Cambridge CB3 7PL, UK.
Tel: 01954-211189
Fax: 01954-211915